Sex, Likes and Social Media

Sex, Likes and Social Media

Talking to our teens
in the digital age

Allison Havey and Deana Puccio

Vermilion
LONDON

1 3 5 7 9 10 8 6 4 2

Vermilion, an imprint of Ebury Publishing,
20 Vauxhall Bridge Road,
London SW1V 2SA

Vermilion is part of the Penguin Random House group of companies whose
addresses can be found at global.penguinrandomhouse.com

Penguin
Random House
UK

First published in the United Kingdom by Vermilion in 2016

www.penguin.co.uk

A CIP catalogue record for this book is available from the British Library

ISBN 9781785040320

Printed and bound in Great Britain by Clays Ltd, St Ives PLC

Penguin Random House is committed to a sustainable
future for our business, our readers and our planet.
This book is made from Forest Stewardship Council®
certified paper.

Contents

Allison's Dedication: Thank you to my family who have remained so supportive of my purpose and passion: Mom and Bob, Dad and Joy and Lisa, Jim, James, Siobhan and Lauren. To my very special, much loved teens, Mike and Isabel. And to Graeme, my partner and best friend. I thank you.

Deana's Dedication: This book is dedicated to my supportive and loving husband Joe who helped me find my way back to doing what I do best, to my beautiful daughters Emily, Abby & Olivia who are the inspiration in my life, and to my Mom, "Big Deana", my role model who always encouraged me to achieve my dreams.

And to all the parents and teenagers struggling to communicate and find a little common ground out there, we hope this book helps.

Foreword

Getting through adolescence is tough, not just for the child growing into the body of a young adult, but for the exhausted and often confused parent. The problems of today's technology-based teenagedom are easier to understand after reading Allison and Deana's book. Who knows what FOMO means? And I know there is a code for 'Red alert, parent approaching' – can someone tell me what it is?

I remember the days when I thought I could monitor what went on in my child's life by joining FB. Feel free to laugh at my naïveté. But what are we parents to do? The dangers our children face are real, even if their worlds may seem virtual. However amazing and useful technology has become we must be vigilant as to how its use (not to mention its addictive lure) affects our children's lives.

From headphones ('too loud, you'll ruin your ears') to pornography (what *is* a teabag?!), we are often at a loss as to how to cope with the new world our children are creating for themselves.

This book and the workshops of RAP can at the very least inform and guide us parents in a calm and intelligent way, giving us key pointers for openers to those tricky but incredibly important conversations we all know we must have with our often inaccessible teenagers.

I am the mother of three children and am extraordinarily proud of them all. They have made courageous decisions and I couldn't be happier when I see the people they have become. The nights spent waiting up for them, the career opportunities wilfully missed in order to be there when they got home from school: I will probably never know if these things made any difference. Whether they are doing well thanks to me or in spite of me will remain one of those maddeningly unanswerable questions but, hopefully, it is a mystical, mysterious mixture of both.

I remember the innocence of my 6 year-olds. That innocence naturally falls away on the road to adulthood, but does it have to be precipitated in this way? Instant access to pornography, to violence (happy slapping?), cutters, haters and trolls? We cannot protect them entirely, nor should we, but we must learn to recognise the danger signs and be able to understand their worries, ask the right questions and encourage their answers. Prepare yourself for the jolt of anger and sadness when you listen to what your child is being subjected to, whether it be bullying, body image obsessions, choices or expectations of sexual behaviour. Then take a deep breath and use the wisdom to be found in this book.

Kristin Scott Thomas

Introduction

You know it's a new dawn when a 17-year-old young woman tells you she is pansexual over a cup of tea, and another explains she prefers to maintain relationships on line as opposed to in person. 'Why?' we ask. 'Because that way I'm not pressured into having sex.' Another young man admits that he is hesitant to go out with a girl in case he is accused of rape. And if he does date someone, 'she might lie about her age' he says. Or when a 13-year-old boy refuses ice cream after a Sunday lunch, explaining: 'I can't eat anything else. I'm working on my six-pack.'

Things have moved on a bit since 2012 when we (Deana Puccio and Allison Havey) founded The RAP Project, an acronym for Raising Awareness and Prevention – and of course 'to rap' also means to communicate. Initially the organisation promoted personal safety and defined rape, sexual assault and consent for teenagers around the UK. Once the rapping started however, it became clear that our teenagers had a lot more on their minds. And wow did they let us know!

As of July 2016, we have brought our RAP Project presentations to over 100 schools and have reached over 16,000 students in England and Scotland, with plans to expand in the very near future to other parts of the UK. Based upon their suggestions and input, our initial 'rap' about personal safety has now expanded to include elements on modern day habits including watching online porn, sexting, social media pressures and 'like spamming'. The insight and willingness to share that we have seen in these young men and women has been eye opening and invaluable.

Yes our audiences initially – just like our own teenagers at home – squirm as we bring up these awkward subjects. But there is an audible sigh of relief in the room once these subjects are finally broached. We have written *Sex, Likes and Social Media: Talking to Our Teens in the Digital Age* so that parents can get a better understanding of what our teenagers are getting up to on- and off-line in a world very different from when we were their age. In addition to the normal biological complications of adolescence, these kids are constantly texting, sexting mad, Facebook frenzied and dealing with a whole new set of rules on dating; and then there's the influence of hard core pornography. 24/7 access to the internet via smartphones allows for a constant stream of porn. According to *Psychologies* magazine, the largest number of online consumers of porn is young men between the ages of 12 and 17. There is no doubt that this has radically influenced how many young men perceive what is 'normal' in sexual relationships.

Hard core porn objectifies women and in many instances promotes rape culture and violence, which, needless to say, neither illustrates nor encourages a consensual, healthy, emotional and physical romantic life. Most teenage girls tell us they are intimidated by how pornography is influencing their relationships and ask us for advice. Many teenage boys have no understanding that there are psychological and physiological repercussions to watching too much porn. But how could they? How can they inherently understand that they are victims of online porn as much as the young women and or young men they are courting? This is why we strongly believe that parents need to start this conversation early on. According to our Rap Project Survey of 2015–16, where we polled a cross-section of 3,000 teens on topics such as pornography, sexting and consent, 83 per cent of young men aged 17–18 (as opposed to 28 per cent of young women in the same age group) have watched porn. Only a third of teenagers asked in the questionnaire ever spoke to one of their parents about their online viewing habits, and how it might unrealistically portray sex. While less than 10 per cent of young women think that watching porn can help them learn about sex, nearly 50 per cent of the older boys think it offers useful pointers in the bedroom.

Additional questions kept resurfacing as our audience was growing. Does social media distort body image? Do teens understand what 'consent' actually means, not just what the legal age is to *give* consent? Is alcohol a date rape drug? What about Rohypnol? What should a student do if they become a victim of sexual assault? Do they understand if they send a sexually explicit image over social media, that it cannot be deleted? And if they are sending a sext under 18, are they breaking the law?

Our kids learn about sex from Sex Education classes in school. But is that enough? It seems that as a culture we have entirely dropped the discussion around personal safety in relationships, around notions of intimacy and the concept of mutual respect and mutual consent. Learning about 'the birds and the bees' in terms of understanding sexuality is out-dated and we are fooling ourselves if we think that this is enough to help teens cope with the challenges they face today.

Between us we have five children: two 19-year-olds, a 16-year-old and two 13-year-olds. There is no doubt that we have dramatically changed our approach to how we address what our older kids did online compared with our younger ones. In fact, we were clueless then as to the effects of social media. Admittedly we missed the boat with our eldest kids. Neither of us had any idea what our older kids got up to online. One friend suggested that Allison's son was most likely watching porn online a few years ago; she was stunned and in total denial. Another asked Deana if her kids ever 'sexted'. 'No way!' she said defensively. But what did we really know? And by the time we had a better grasp of what was happening out there in our sweet children's secret society in cyberspace, they were adults too, and too old to discuss it with us. We were parenting based upon our own personal experiences of being teenagers.

How could we understand what it's like to receive a naked photo of another 14-year-old on our phone or be influenced by watching hard core pornography late at night? The door was well and truly shut. But, with our younger kids, we are better prepared to speak to them about WhatsApp, Snapchat and Instagram, who their followers *actually* are and whether these images and texts are appropriate or not. Regarding porn, many kids stumble upon hard core images that can confuse and frighten them. Let's talk to them *before* this happens, and ask them to tell us if they see something that concerns them. Just because the media normalises misogyny, themes of male domination and 'laddism', doesn't mean that our kids have to drink the kool-aid. When prime time family shows like *The X Factor* feature Rhianna stripped down to high heels, fish-nets, mini shorts and a bra-top, we may want to tell our kids that this might not be the best way to showcase one's vocal skills. When adverts feature four male models dominating a scantily clad woman in order to sell jeans, it might be good to analyse the story the advert is actually telling (hint: it's not a good one). This is not prudishness, nor are we being overly moral or didactic; it is a simple fact that as parents we need to acknowledge that many of these images are too complex for young minds to process, without those minds wanting to then emulate what they see.

Are these subliminal images and messages leading to a rise in sexual violence? Are they influencing relationships in an unhealthy way? The Office of National Statistics reported in 2014 that rape cases are up 29 per cent, while sexual assaults are up 21 per cent in England and Wales; all other violent crime was down.

We started researching personal safety courses focusing on these issues. Did schools or community centres address any of them? While we did find physical self-defence lessons and victim aftercare programmes, we could not find anything focusing on prevention. In our opinion, if you are in the position of having to physically protect yourself, it is too late. There was nothing out there teaching common sense skills to our teens or empowering them to own their bodies and choices. Having spoken with heads of schools, heads of PSHE and Pastoral Care departments, they agreed that they just didn't have time in their curriculum to include a programme with as much detail as we envisioned. Additionally, it can be awkward for a teacher to talk about sex so openly in one lesson and then have to teach maths in the next. This is something that, as outsiders, we felt we could do.

And why us? Other than being concerned mothers of teenagers, we have some experience in these areas professionally. Deana, a lawyer, spent her legal career as a Sex Crimes Prosecutor in Brooklyn, New York. And Allison is a TV journalist and news producer who reported on stories like this from all over the world. Our friends found Deana's stories of crimes scenes and investigations compelling. Maybe we could speak to teenagers and parents in the same way? We felt that by basing our presentations on real-life cases that we worked or reported on, we could let these examples illustrate how a choice made in a certain situation can change the rest of your life. Our goal is for the teens to listen to our examples and come to their own conclusions about their behaviour. One of our favourite lines is that 'we are not preaching morality but teaching reality'.

Despite some parents' initial shock at our mission, everyone seems to be asking the same question: Why aren't these subjects being talked about *more* in schools?

The reality is that when we bring our New York accents into a hall filled with teenagers, nervous giggles and snickers quickly dissolve into rapt attention. This has less to do with us having super powers and everything to do with the fact that teens really want to discuss the issues of sexual assault, consent, how porn today influences sexuality and relationships, and why misogyny is playing such an unwelcome role at schools and universities.

When in 2013 The Home Office, the Ministry of Justice and the Office for National Statistics put together their first-ever joint official statistics bulletin on sexual violence called *An Overview of Sexual Offending in England and Wales*, the researchers found that approximately 85,000 women were sexually assaulted or raped every year. According to the then Deputy Prime Minister Nick Clegg, while addressing the issue of sexual assault, the understanding is that approximately 250,000 women are sexually assaulted each year but do not file police reports. And according to the NSPCC, 35 per cent of all sexual assaults recorded in England and Wales in 2012–13 were sexual crimes against children under 16.

We also feel obligated to share a report published by The Children's Society in 2015; it doesn't make for pleasant reading. The charity found that police in England recorded 4,900 sexual offence cases – including sexual exploitation, rape and sexual assaults – amongst 16 and 17-year-olds in the last year. The report shows that half of young people who did not report such crimes took that course of action because they did not consider it worth reporting, feared going to court, or did not want the perpetrators punished. The organisation's analysis of the Crime Survey for England and Wales revealed that an estimated 50,000 girls of this age say they have been victims of these crimes. That's a staggering number of unreported cases and unheard voices.

Finally, with our access, we wanted to understand some of our audiences' behaviour and concerns. RAP undertook a survey of 3,000 teenagers aged between 13 and 18. We separated our teens by age groups of 13–14, 15–16 and 17–18 and by gender. Some of the questions included: *Do you watch porn online? Have you ever spoken to a parent about porn? Have you ever sent a sext?*

The teenagers were united in their top concern, irrespective of age or gender, then varied according to age and gender:

- Number one concern for all: Exams/School Work
- Number two concern for Boys aged 15–16 & 17–18: Sex
- Number two concern for Boys aged 13–14: Body Image
- Number two concern for Girls aged 17–18: Social Life/Friendships
- Number two concern for Girls 13–14; 15–16: Body Image
- Number three concern for Girls 17–18 & for Boys 15–16; 17–18: Future
- Number three concern for Boys 13–14 & for Girls 15–16: Social Life/Friendships

Our presentations are meant to empower teenagers. By speaking candidly about these very real, very challenging and at times awkward subjects, we hope we are opening the door to honest and frank discussions between parents and their kids. What we can offer to parents who read this book is a direct line into the minds of their teenagers and of the struggles they face every day. We want this book to spark a discussion between you and your teen, and we hope to help you in having those discussions. We believe that awareness is power and hope that by reading this book you will not only be more aware of these issues, but also feel more confident to help your teen navigate their life in the digital age.

1 How Relationships Have Changed

'I met a guy at a nearby school in Tunbridge Wells. Justin and I shared mutual friends. He had a great personality and, to be frank, he was FIT. I liked him immediately. We hit it off, flirted, and he asked me for my number and email address. What followed next was not ideal. Rather than actually talk, he initiated our romance by text. Finally, he asked me on a date. Via text. I made an effort to look good on that Friday night and waited for him to tell me where and when we were meeting. Justin finally texted, and asked me for my Skype address. This guy actually wanted our hot date to take place on Skype! I mean, how much effort is a walk around town and a beer? I gave up on guys for a while after that.'

Amelie, sixth form student, Kent

Watching 'The Way We Was'* episode of *The Simpsons* recently, we were genuinely touched by the sweet but somewhat prehistoric storyline. The episode first aired in 1991 and described a flashback to 1974 when Homer first saw Marge in the final year of high school and fell in love at first sight. Summoning all of his courage, he invited Marge to be his date for the prom. As

---

* Twelfth episode of the second season of *The Simpsons*. It originally aired on the Fox network in the United States on 31 January 1991.

in this episode, beautiful dresses, sharp suits, corsages and a limousine were a few of the key prom elements. Often, the man would arrive at the young lady's house in a borrowed or hired car to collect her for the dance. The bell rings, the door opens and the parents have an opportunity to size up the young man at the door. With comic wit, the *Simpsons'* cartoonists immediately let the viewer know by the parents' facial expressions that Homer just doesn't make the grade. Adding insult to injury, Marge was completely taken aback by Homer's arrival. She had forgotten her promise to be on his arm for the night and had said yes to a preferred suitor. The doorbell rings again. A distinguished young man is at the door, warmly received. The parents drool over this guy. Superficially, he is articulate with a far more promising future. The comic twist is that Marge had inadvertently said yes to two dates, and opts to leave poor lovesick Homer on his own. But the date goes terribly wrong and she ends the evening with Homer. True love at last.

Looking at Amelie's experience against the story of how Homer and Marge met we can see a genuine, if dramatic, reflection on how relationships and dating habits have changed over the past 40 years. *The Simpsons'* story may seem sentimental, but for decades this is how many parents met their teenagers' first sweethearts. While proms have only recently arrived in the UK they have been part of the American coming-of-age moment for decades; there was barely a single teen movie in the eighties that didn't have a prom scene.

Let's get some perspective on how meeting our romantic partners has dramatically transformed over the years. At the turn of the twentieth century, women had little, if any, freedom. The ritual of courtship in western societies could not have been further away from the present day. Dating was a far more formal arrangement that was carefully planned by parents or family friends. Chaperones were nearly always present to oversee the couple in case of any impropriety. In some cases, marriages were arranged. But once the roaring twenties took hold, elaborate beaded dresses replaced restrictive corsets and suddenly a sexual liberation took hold. Writer Amanda Chatel made some astute observations in her article for .Mic in 2014, entitled 'How the "First Date" Has Changed in Every Decade Through History'. She explains how the dawn of cinema, automobiles and prohibition created an era of adventure and sexuality in the twenties. Couples could canoodle in the darkened movie halls or, if fortunate enough to own a car, drive away from prying parental guidance. She writes, 'Indeed, "playing the field" by dating multiple people became more common in this decade, as the liberated women we now know as "flappers" explored sexual boundaries and brought taboos like premarital sex out of the closet.' But with the onset of the Second World War and its draft of young, eligible men, women faced a supply shortage of the opposite sex. The urgency in finding a suitor and obtaining a 'promise' from a soldier setting off for the war took hold, giving hope to both parties during a difficult and dangerous time. 'Going steady' gained popularity in the fifties, with more women attending university. Sad but true, this was a sure-fire way for many to meet the man of their dreams, a 'lifelong hook-up' of sorts. Often academics were pushed aside with the aim of instead becoming engaged to a coed. Allison's mother met her husband at a college basketball game. She watched him run around the court, skilfully sink some baskets and, hey presto, love blossomed post match. He asked her out on a date that day which led to dances, drive-ins and diners. After going steady for a while, they married. But then the sixties and seventies saw the birth of free love, the pill, acceptance of premarital sex and the women's liberation movement. Sexual intimacy was part of the 'getting to know you' process. Enter the excessive eighties ... Apart from those in stable and monogamous relationships, many others indulged in adultery. Suddenly finding a man to come home to became that much tougher. When a book entitled, *The Rules: Time-tested Secrets for Capturing the Heart of Mr. Right* was published by two New Yorkers Ellen Fein and Sherrie Schneider in 1995, copies flew off the shelves. The fundamental tenet of *The Rules* is that a woman is 'easy to be with but hard to get'. Let the man pursue you, never pursue the man, urge the love gurus. A close friend, who has been happily married for over 20 years, is proud to admit she followed this self-help book's suggestions and, in the end, her fellow put a ring on it. Interestingly enough, the two authors came under a lot of criticism for their black and white, formulaic approach. That, however, did not stop them from writing an update on digital dating for singletons. Fein and Schneider's most recent book *Not Your Mother's Rules: The New Secrets for Dating* transfers the rule of 'Never call the man first' to 'Never answer a man's ad first'. They advise that if a Match.com man doesn't ask you out within four emails, delete and move on! 'Rules women want dates not pen pals,' the women write. This is a very brief synopsis of the history of dating over the past 100 years, but we think revisiting these habits is valuable. Imagine how our grandparents felt when our parents began swinging in the late sixties and seventies. Probably similar to how we feel now with our own children as they embark on liaisons via Facebook, sexting and social media.

Whatever Happened to 'Old-fashioned' Dating?

We started dating in the eighties. Dances, movies and concerts were the romantic order of the day. But boy have relationships changed! Many of our kids will meet their first date online rather than in person. Today's teens' love lives are on steroids: online flirting, sexting, Skype sex, Tinder and Grindr are all the rage.

After speaking to teenage girls and boys around the country and reading the newspapers here and in the US, there is no doubt that social media has replaced, for a large part, the personal art of 'courting'. During our RAP Project presentations, we like to talk about an age-old formula for relationships; 'Friendship, Romance and Intimacy'. Nearly all of the students look absolutely dumbfounded when we say these words, yet are eager to hear more. One head teacher at a prominent school, who applauded our work and booked us for three more sessions the following term, thought this 'formula' concept on relationships might be a little too 'old-fashioned'.

We don't think so. Why don't we remind our kids that this is how it used to work? A friendship develops, then romance blossoms and then one thing leads to another. So many teenagers today use porn as a sex manual rather than an open, intimate conversation between two people who care for each other. What a bad idea. Today's porn is pretty hard core and its love-making techniques have a lot to answer for. (We will discuss this in much more detail in Chapter Five (page 91).). At Boston College, Professor Kerry Cronin is teaching a philosophy class where traditional dating is part of the syllabus. She developed this after a student some years earlier had asked her if she had ever been on a date. Taken aback, she began researching the premise that young people did not date because they actually did not know *how* to date. Dating for many teenagers today is unfamiliar, she maintains. Professor Cronin refers to this trend as a 'lost social script'. How are her students expected to ask someone out on a date if their peer group is not doing it? And once they get their courage up, what do they say? If the date takes, where do they go? What do they talk about? How do they engage on a deeper level? Would asking a person out on a date appear 'cringy' or 'weird'? Our kids are out of practice. As our teens spend so much time online, the art of conversation is a dying one. On top of this, leaving the house and actually going out on a date takes time and planning. This generation of teenagers are used to instant gratification. Why go to the cinema and spend £15 when you can stay in and illegally download a film for free? How can young people build a romantic relationship on a foundation built online?

Back in Professor Cronin's class, the university students are given dating assignments dictating a strict list of rules that students must abide by. These include:

- A date lasting between 60 and 90 minutes
- A student must ask out the other person face-to-face, not via text or any other form of social media
- No kissing, sex or alcohol consumption permitted

Her aim with this academic task is to bring dating back to its bare, personal essentials and avoid hiding behind a screen or using alcohol to fuel confidence to negotiate a social situation. First year student Frank Dimartino told a journalist, 'It's easy to hook up with someone you've just met in a dark room. But asking someone out on a date in broad daylight? Now that's scary.' What is disconcerting is the trend towards what we believe is an aggressive, highly unromantic approach to romantic love. This may be at a party, in a park, in a schoolyard or even in the loo at the local Starbucks.

Fifteen-year-old Lilly shared a story that took place at a house party. She was chatting to a young man named John who she knew tangentially as they were 'friends' on Facebook. During a quiet conversation away from the crowd, Lilly and John were deep in conversation about mutual school friends, exams and what they enjoyed doing on weekends. Fran, a schoolmate of Lilly's, brushed rudely in-between them and spoke rather loudly into the young man's ear. 'Do you want to get off with me?' she asked. The guy could hardly believe his luck, smiled and walked away with this eager, attractive girl. Lilly felt abandoned, double-crossed and rather shocked at her friend's behaviour. She wondered why she should bother to have a conversation and get to know someone if, at the end of the day, there is no point. It is a lot less hurtful to have a relationship with John over a social media site than in real life.

We know, of course, that some teens do go out to the movies or on dinner dates, but, more often than not, these romantic pastimes have been replaced by gatherings of some sort, be they in a park or at a house party. Between the ages of 13 and 16 (Years 9 and 10) appears to be when this really starts gaining momentum and the experimentation begins. There may be some alcohol or some pot smoking involved. If there is an attraction between two people, the young lovebirds might walk off somewhere private and make out, or more.

The 'Hook-up' Generation

Writer and astute social observer Tom Wolfe notes in his book aptly named *Hooking Up* that the widely-used phrase of 'hook-up' went mainstream by 2000. Most parents understood it to mean to meet up and hang out. Some years later it came to mean to kiss. Thanks to the cultural influences of TV shows like *Made in Chelsea*, we parents are now even more confused as 'hook-up' can mean a whole variety of sexual experiences from deep kissing and oral sex to full intercourse. Wolfe reminds us that American girls had used baseball terminology to describe sexual adventures in the following way: 'first base' referred to kissing; 'second base' referred to fondling and deep, or 'French', kissing; 'third base' referred to fellatio or oral sex; and 'home plate' was going 'all the way'. But by the year 2000, in the era of hooking up, Wolfe only half-heartedly joked that third base jumps to full sex while a 'home plate' meant learning each other's names.

The lack of information our teens have about a romantic interest can lead them into serious trouble. A 17-year-old male student, let's call him Ben, from Essex, shared his story of meeting a young woman at a party. Emma did not attend his school. Ben noticed her immediately, noting her sexy, cool sense of fashion. They began talking, and he asked her how old she was. 'Sixteen,' she replied. They shared a few beers and then stepped outside for a walk. One thing led to another and they 'hooked up'. They exchanged first names and mobile numbers. Over the next few weeks, they stayed in touch but his interest waned. He had met someone at his own school and felt he should break off contact with Emma, which he considered a casual date of some sorts. He texted her, explaining he had met someone else and could no longer stay in contact with her. Within moments, he received a text threatening him with criminal action. 'I lied to you. I am only 14 years old and what you did with me was against the law.' He freaked out and could not believe this woman was only 14! He remembered the mature way she carried herself. 'No friggin' way!' he thought. He could not believe he was so stupid to assume she was 16 or older based entirely on her appearance. Having no idea what to do, he turned to his teacher who in turn explained the situation to the head of school. The head then contacted her counterpart at Emma's school and further crisis was avoided without police involvement. Whenever Allison tells this story, there are inevitably some shocked and horrified expressions from the males in the audience; it is a useful tale to tell, especially in this age of casual sex. Ben suffered embarrassment, shame and real fear of criminal action. He said he would never be so careless again and insisted that we share his story with as many teenage boys as possible. And we do. One boy asked Deana if he should ask a girl for ID if he fancied her. What we suggest is getting to know the person a bit better, knowing their age, first and last names, as well as their school. Maybe go on a date or two before 'hooking up' with someone. Or take the slower 'Friendship, Romance, Intimacy' route, which prevents this type of situation entirely. Otherwise, our sons – and, in rarer cases, our daughters – could get a criminal record.

One confident, well-spoken 17-year-old young man named Jack described to us a typical party environment in London 2015: the guys were stoned or drinking vodka, and the girls had taken great pains to look stunning, wearing make-up and, in most cases, revealing clothes. Jack observed that young women are really suffering from high levels of insecurity and low self-esteem, and he and his mates have no idea why. 'They are gorgeous. They are smart. Yet what they will do for our attention ... Literally, all a guy has to do nowadays to hook up with a girl is to take a shower and comb his hair. Really.' This we find incredibly sad. Is our society creating a group of young people who think that their only self-worth is sexual?

Girlguiding UK publishes its Girls' Attitudes Survey every year. The questionnaires address issues including sexual harassment, self-harm, self-esteem and body image. The 2015 survey asked 1,574 girls aged between 7 and 21 about the state of their mental health. Girlguiding Chief Executive, Julie Bentley, described the results as a 'stark warning about the fragile state of UK girls' well-being'. Self-harm was the biggest health concern, and 82 per cent said adults often failed to recognise the intense pressures they are under. About a third said they were concerned over their own mental health. Two in five of the girls said they have been victims of a demeaning comment made to them about the way they look. These surveys are extremely valuable to parents, offering an inside view on girls' top concerns.

Twenty-first Century Pressures

The RAP Project is very grateful to have the eyes and ears of thousands of teenagers but they also have a lot to say. In the autumn/winter of 2015–16, we surveyed 3,000 students between the ages of 14 and 18 and asked them to describe some of their biggest concerns. In no particular order, exams, body image, romance, finding a job after university and fear of sexual assault topped the list. The students we speak to, on a stress scale of 1–10, are hitting new highs. Faced with a real competitive desire to get high marks and a physical desire to look 'perfect' – complete with thigh gap, six-pack and literally topped and tailed with a Kim Kardashian bum and chest – alongside a natural desire to be well liked, how can they not be? But here's the twist: social media is 24/7. Flirting on the sports field or fighting in the cafeteria no longer ends at the school gates at 4pm – it carries on *all* day, *all* evening and, at times, *all* night ... online. These online discussions are often vacuous, insatiable and can be extremely vicious. Imagine the stress of carrying an argument online all evening? Or the pressure of looking lovely and fresh through the early hours online, then getting up and out for school early the same day?

If there is one word we try to hit home to the kids we speak to, it is DISCRETION. Practise it. Use it. Love it. Do not stray from it. Be discreet. No one is obligated to respond to every WhatsApp, Instagram, FaceTime, Facebook or text message. But with regards to relationships and social media, things can quickly spin out of control. Practising discretion is essential.

Encourage your child to refrain from responding to everything that is sent to them: there is no obligation to 'Like' a photo. Advise them to not share personal information about their romantic relationships with more than their most trusted, closest friends, and maybe not to put these private situations in writing online at all. Nothing beats face-to-face contact and conversation – there are fewer misunderstandings and often more opportunities to build a friendship that way. Secrets are private and, if an argument ensues, online footprints can be forwarded to anyone, damaging a blossoming romance or even a person's mental well-being. (We speak much more on this issue later in Chapter Four.)

Back to Jack, who described to us just how much pressure students are under. He says there is no doubt this pressure affects relationships today. 'At best,' he said, 'relationships last about a month. We have such heavy workloads that it is just not possible to maintain them.' He adds that 'dating is too much of a headache', asking 'who has time for romance? Social media is like a spider's web of gossip and lies. Your entire personal life is online, fiction or otherwise, when you are involved with someone. Hook-ups are much easier.'

Keeping in mind all of the above pressures faced by young people, compounded by the complexities of social media, many teenagers are bound to suffer from self-esteem issues and anxieties. And we've barely even touched on pornography yet. The RAP Project believes that hard core porn, sexting and social media in general is distorting, manipulating and preventing healthy relationships. For the first time, we have a generation of teenagers who are using Internet porn to learn about sex. Thirty-five years ago, we may remember looking through *Penthouse* and *Playboy* magazines, or maybe watching an art house movie like *Emmanuelle*, but you probably agree that these are hardly examples of modern day porn. Just one example, Gonzo Porn portrays women having sex with misogynistic men intent on control rather than sensual intimacy. Teenagers are clearly getting the wrong idea here and are suffering from confusing messages. Our desire to promote healthier relationships and to send home our message of 'Friendship, Romance and Intimacy' really is not an easy one to fulfil. In Chapter Five we speak in much more detail on how porn is influencing this generation.

In the spring of 2015, we took our teenagers to see a powerful play called *Four Minutes Twelve Seconds*. Written by playwright James Fritz, the play tells the story of a young man in the midst of A levels with a promising future studying law at Durham University. The tight family unit is torn apart when a home-made sex video starring their son and a young woman comes to light online. Questions including 'Who posted the video?' and 'Is the sex consensual?' fly furiously throughout the play. The story hits topical issues head-on, including the power and influence of porn, the meaning of consent, criminal accountability, honesty and intimacy in relationships. It's well worth seeing or, if that's not possible, it's definitely worth a read.

The pressure of sex

We have had several long conversations about relationships with one of our work experience interns, 16-year-old Talia Fogelman. Talia explained that there is immense pressure on girls to 'put out' today from young men. Speaking to a gay male teenager, he reports back that he does not feel this same pressure as his female counterparts. Why do women feel obliged to be physically intimate, on any level, with a guy they are not yet close to? Talia blames a large part of this on the media. 'The media creates certain ideas around relationships. This is totally centred around sex. As a result, we fear that if we do not have sexual relations, we will be dumped. Sex is our value.'

Despite the peer pressure to have sex, there is a massive disconnect between highly sexualised youth and the danger of damaging one's reputation. Talia adds, 'Guys are very quick to talk about sex, to brag about it. And the more a girl does, the more appealing she is.' But to the girls, she is considered 'loose, slutty'. Girls do brag about some of their performances but tend to be more discreet than the boys. Guys tend to talk so much about sex and focus on details such as penis size. There is an equation between men and their sexual prowess. 'I've overheard teenage boys comparing their penis sizes with each other, bragging indiscreetly about how much sex they have had, how much they are "getting with" girls. They seem to believe the more sex they have, the more appealing and macho they are. When in fact many girls think it is quite sleazy,' says Talia. Again, you may shake your head and say well nothing much has changed since we were teenagers: boys want to have sex and brag about it and girls feel pressured to have sex of some sort to be liked. However, the problem is not that young people are having sex. We believe the problem is that our kids are becoming sexualised much earlier, and at the same time, being introduced to considerably more mature sexual practices.

As parents we are realistic that one day our kids will be sexually active. 'When?' is the question we ask and we hope that, when they do, they will act responsibly with regards to birth control and protection against STDs. All teenagers mature at different times, and some may not be sexually active until they are in their twenties. But this is not what worries us. What worries us is the 13-year-old boy who comes up to us at the end of a RAP presentation and quietly asks us the following: 'Miss, sodomy, you know, anal sex, is not "real" sex right? You don't have to be 16 to consent to that do you?' And we care about the 15-year-old girl who is pressured into having sex without discussion just because she has done it once before. This is precisely why it is crucial that we discuss what consent actually means. So many young people, both male and female, incorrectly think that if they have done something sexual before, it means they have to do it again. First we ask students, 'What is the age of consent?' Everyone in every school knows the answer is 16. But when we probe further and ask them to define consent, they fall silent. This is why we want to educate our children about consent, rape and hard core pornography (which blurs the lines so dangerously). We want them to feel empowered and confident enough to discuss intimacy. We always tell our students, if they are old enough to have sex, they are old enough to talk about what they are going to do first with their partner. If two young people practise mutual respect and mutual consent, then the friendship is ready for the next step: intimacy. This first love can set the foundation for future relationships, and hopefully healthy, happy ones.

Sexual orientation

There's also another layer to our teenagers' sexuality. Once, people were identified as either straight, gay, bisexual or homosexual. We remember our gay friends barely spoke of their sexuality, many remaining in the closet until well into university. But these days things are far more 'fluid'. According to a poll conducted by YouGov in 2015, more than half do not see themselves as either straight or gay, refusing to be labelled with any specific sexual preferences. Today's additional sexual orientations include pansexual, gender fluid and polysexual. The YouGov survey shows that with each generation, more people are choosing against defining a sexual orientation. Our children are growing up with role models including Kristen Stewart and Cara Delevingne. Both women are open about their relationships, be they with men or women. Supporters say the new sexual compass points to the person, not the gender. Whether Caitlyn Jenner made it a talking point or not, transgender is definitely a part of a bigger sexual dialogue today. One 14-year-old girl named Abigail told us, 'Transgender and gay rights are my generation's cause.'

Whatever one's preferences, teenagers today are telling us they are confused, angry and disappointed about relationships. There is no doubt they need clear definitions of consent, as well as a better understanding of what is influencing the expectations, attitudes and body image of both young men and women.

ROMANCE

Relationships: remember 'Friendships, Romance and Intimacy'

Offline courtship is more fun than online communication

Make love not porn

Avoid hook-ups. They can prove problematic

Not everyone matures sexually simultaneously

Concerns? Share them with someone you trust

Equality: respect gender identity and sexual preferences

TOP TIPS

- Encourage your teens to talk about romantic relationships
- Discuss consent and what it means. More than once
- Remind your teen that having sex is one thing, but how one feels afterwards can be altogether different

Resources

One in two young people say they are not 100% Heterosexual

https://yougov.co.uk/news/2015/08/16/
half-young-not-heterosexual/

Disrespect NoBody

www.disrespectnobody.co.uk/

Girlguiding

http://new.girlguiding.org.uk

The RAP (Raising Awareness and Prevention) Project

www.therapproject.co.uk

2 Dealing With Unwanted Attention

'On Wednesday after school a girl in the senior school was approached by a stranger in Belsize Park. The police have been informed and are actively looking for the perpetrator. The girls were informed this afternoon in registration and once again given advice about their personal safety and what to do in such a situation. Please remind your daughters to be vigilant and to call the police immediately on 999 if they feel threatened or uncomfortable in any way.'

Excerpt from a letter sent via email to parents
from a north London school in 2015

Unsettling, to say the least. Is there a communal, pervasive fear of letting our children walk or get a train or bus to school, to town, to a shop or to a friend's house? Is this normal? When do we stop worrying? An 85-year-old friend of Allison's says this concern remains a constant even when your children become adults, so we should get used to it! A few decades ago, no one thought twice of their child jumping on their bike or walking to a friend's house. Did parents even bat an eyelid? Nowadays all of us at one time or another have told our sons or daughters to ignore strangers if they speak to them, to cross to the other side of the street if they see a white van or to avoid walking alone.

Unwanted attention happens to most kids, from about the age of 11 or 12, when they are changing physically and emotionally. One 17-year-old man we know described his change into manhood as if it appeared magnified and progressed in 'slow motion'. One 14-year-old girl recalled the transition as if 'every cell was bursting with life, yet lost in chaotic confusion'. This phase, in which kids hurtle towards adolescence, is pubescence, and it is an age group The Rap Project feels obligated to start paying more attention to, in addition to teenagers. Why? Because we speak to parents and teachers nearly every day of the school year and more and more are suggesting we speak to children in Years Five and Six in primary school. This seems to be because children as young as 10 or 11 are now becoming sexualised thanks to advertising. movies, TV programmes, music videos, music lyrics and, of course, online pornography. And while they may digest the visual, they are too young to emotionally come to terms with its repercussions. In this chapter, we want to address how children transitioning into adolescents and teenagers should deal with unwanted attention and we will share some advice we have learned from our own experience, other parents, teens and from other organisations.

No one spoke to us as kids about how to handle unwanted attention and, for the most part, young people experience it and move on. But why not calmly discuss that a situation may arise at this transitional age with your child? People may act inappropriately, but it is not our children's fault. We believe these pre-adolescents and teens need to ask for help or at least feel comfortable enough to talk about an incident if it occurs. As we have all read about in too many news accounts, many children who are victims of unwanted sexual advances remain silent until adulthood.

The reality is that children, most often from the age of 10 and older, start to sense an awkward sexual awareness or encounter an unwelcome sexual experience. 'Flashers', 'gropers' and/or 'lewd comments' are just some of the things that children can be on the receiving end of. Wikipedia defines 'indecent exposure' as taking place 'in circumstances where the exposure is contrary

26

to local moral or other standards of appropriate behaviour. Social and community attitudes to the exposing of various body parts and laws covering what is referred to as indecent exposure vary significantly in different countries. It ranges from prohibition of exposure of genital areas, buttocks, and female breasts. Not all countries have indecent exposure laws.'

As two New York kids back in the day, we vividly remember flashers standing on some of the large boulders in Central Park, shamelessly revealing their shockingly pale white, naked bodies in the middle of winter to joggers and passengers in cars. Flashers are found everywhere in the world, yet prosecution is rare. The crime is considered a sexual assault, but, unless the police see the person in the actual act of indecently exposing him or herself, there are no grounds for arrest.

A 17-year-old girl shared the following story with us. A developing 12-year-old Sally and her mother Ellen were Christmas shopping on Oxford Street. The street was teeming with people carrying bags laden with gifts, and the heavy footfall meant the crowd moved slowly towards the tube or shops. Sally felt uncomfortable amid the crowds and wanted to go home. Her mum asked her to please hang in there for one more item on the shopping list. As they waited for the lights to turn green at Oxford Circus, Sally felt something pressing against her bum. Assuming this awkward pressure was a shopping bag belonging to the person behind her, she shifted her weight and moved to the left. The 'bag' remained attached to her bum. With so many shoppers in the street, she convinced herself it was someone's bag. She moved to the right, and so did the object pressing on her bum. Suddenly, she went cold. She turned around and saw a man staring at her. She knew it was his hand that was on her bum. 'Mum, don't look but someone is touching me.' Her mother turned around and saw a middle-aged man staring intensely at her young daughter. She quickly grabbed Sally's arm and marched briskly in the opposite direction. After a minute, Sally turned around. The man had walked in her direction and stood still, his eyes boring into her.

Sally felt scared, sick and angry that this man had felt her up, showed no remorse and had got away with it.

Pat Bacchus, who trains rape counsellors and runs Victim Support Barnet in north London, can empathise. She was flashed at the age of 14. 'It is a form of sexual assault,' she says. 'It's distasteful, it's intimidating, it's violating the woman. It's the same whether he touches her or not.' Her latest such encounter occurred en route to Scotland Yard to discuss rape counselling with police chiefs. She and a female colleague were standing on the platform waiting for the Tube: 'I turned around and there was a boy – he couldn't have been more than 15 years old – swinging his penis in the air! I said to my colleague, "You're not going to believe this". There he stood, enjoying the glance of a woman. And in such a public place! I thought, "How has he got the nerve to risk it?"'

Responding to Unwanted Attention

We think it could be valuable to share what we discuss with the students in this section.

One of the many slides we share in our Social Skills presentation with the younger year groups – Years 8–10 specifically – deals with precisely this type of 'unwanted attention'. Speaking to boys and girls, either mixed or in single sex groups, we elicit how the students would react to different scenarios:

WHAT WOULD YOU DO?

A. Man exposes himself to you in a park.

B. Unwanted touching by a stranger on a crowded bus.

C. If you are going into a chat room online and a man or a woman shows his or her private parts.

Here are some of the reactions to scenario A:

- 'I would scream and run in the opposite direction.'
- 'I would ignore him, mind my own business and walk quickly on my way.'
- 'I would find a policeman or an adult and explain what I have seen.'
- 'Using my smartphone, I would record a few seconds of his actions or take a photo of him and show it to the police as evidence.'
- 'I would punch him.'

What is our advice? Well we quickly discount the latter option, as violence is never the answer. We explain that you never know the mental state of the person, be it a classic 'flasher' getting his or her thrill for attention or an escapee from a psychiatric ward with violent tendencies. Walking in the opposite direction and reporting the incident to a police officer or an adult you trust is always the safest choice.

A mature Year 10 student shared his story of taking a bus home rather late one night after attending a party. 'I was taking the night bus home around 12.30am. The bus was empty. I was listening to music with my headphones. The bus stopped and a man got on and, despite all the other empty seats, chose to sit next to me. I felt annoyed but carried on minding my own business. When the bus moved, he began poking me. I removed my headphones and he asked me for the time. I told him, and once again listened to my music. I felt deeply uncomfortable but decided to simply ignore him if he bothered me again. Why didn't I move seats? I don't know why. I thought it might be rude. After a few minutes, he began rubbing my inner thigh. I stood up, which luckily grabbed the bus driver's attention. The driver sussed out what was going on, pulled over and demanded the man get off the bus. I got home safely but felt pretty freaked out.'

Here are some responses we have heard from students when asking them to consider how they would react in a similar situation in scenario B:

- 'If someone was obviously touching me inappropriately, I would angrily tell him to stop, back off and get out of my personal space.'
- 'I would get off the bus and take the next one.'
- 'Scream and kick him where it hurts.'

Again, we explain that kicking is not an option unless it is the absolute last resort, as the offender could have a knife or other weapon and grow violent. What we do recommend is, if it is daylight and the child feels able to do so, to get off the bus and take the next one of course if your child sees the perpetrator following them off the bus or train, they need to stick on the transport and move as closely as possible to the driver or other people. The key is to not get isolated.

The best solution if at all possible is to move away from the 'perv' and get the attention of the driver or other passengers so that you can get help and report what has happened. But, if it is late at night, as in this student's case, we advise the victim to grab the driver's attention as soon as possible. Remind your child that it's important to sit as close as possible to the driver if the bus is empty.

Having spoken to members of law enforcement in both the UK and the US they tell us to remind our kids that their safety is paramount. However, they also feel it is important for your child to take control back from the perpetrator and establish clear boundaries. If, based on their circumstances, your child feels secure enough to say something, police recommend children should say things like:

- 'Stop touching me.'
- 'I don't know you.'
- 'Stay away from me.'

Heidi E. Mason, a senior assistant District Attorney in New York, makes a very valuable point: 'Because of the multitude of cultural and social issues, your teenager would not want to get hysterical or enrage the abuser. For instance, you would not want to raise your voice to a man if you are a female tourist visiting a more conservative country. Staying calm is the most important thing, stating clearly in a steady voice, "Do not touch me, move away". Advise your child to move towards another adult and move away.'

After one of our presentations a girl in Year 8 asked us privately for advice on how to handle a repeating situation she was finding very tricky to deal with. 'I have a friend who I really like to spend time with. We have a great laugh, and she is a loyal friend at school. Recently, however, I have been going over to her house and things are weird. We normally get a snack and then hang out in her room with the door closed. She was really excited one day to show me this new online chat room she had been visiting. The other people who visited this chat room were her age, she said, with similar interests. You didn't see the person in the chat room unless you both clicked a window allowing a two- or three-way more personal chat. The first time we did this together, a man was playing with his penis in close up. The second time we did this a man asked us to take off our tops. I hate going on this chat room as I find these people gross. But she seems to get a thrill. I don't want to lose her friendship, but I feel she should stop going on this site. It is wrong, even dangerous. If I tell my mum, she will tell my friend's mum and I will be labelled a telltale. And if I tell our other friends at school, they too may think I am "weird" for visiting these sites. What do I do?'

Here are some students' comments about how they would react if someone in a chat room exposed themselves, as in scenario C:

- 'I would close down the chat and report the person to the administration on the website.'

- 'I would delete the history of the website and never, ever go on this site again.'
- 'I would tell my mum or dad.'

Any one of the above would be an appropriate response.

One of the reasons we founded The RAP Project was in recognition of these new, unpredictable online scenarios. The number of stories we have gathered from parents and students are too numerous to detail in this book. Gaming and fake identities through avatars, fake personas on chat rooms and how kids can be the victim of highly sexual language or body part exposure seems to be growing at an alarming rate. And so many of these sites can be infiltrated by paedophiles. As parents, we can either trust our children to have the maturity to deal with whatever they may come across or supervise which sites they visit. Realistically, we will not be able to prevent what they see at school or while visiting friends, but we can talk to them about what to do if someone behaves inappropriately online:

- Log off
- Close the chat down
- Tell an adult
- Report someone if he or she has behaved criminally

We go much more into online safety in the next chapter (page 49).

Having discussed flashers, gropers and unexpected online sexual exposure to the students we address, we thought we had the basics pretty well covered. But then a parent wrote to us with this rather complex situation. Again, the proliferation and obsession with social media had added yet another complex layer to an already complicated childhood.

Here is an excerpt from her email with regards to a Year 7 girl at an independent school:

'I have become increasingly concerned about the online behaviour of a girl in my daughter's year. She has posted a few very inappropriate photos and has something like 900 followers, many of them older men from different countries. I don't know her parents and it may well be that she has numerous accounts and they are unaware of what is going on. I don't feel comfortable with knowing about but not acting on her behaviour. Not only does it raise child protection issues about the girl herself (as well as the issue of why she is behaving like this) but all these followers can clearly see her uniform and can easily identify the school and its location. So there are wider implications here. Given that I have never spoken to her parents, the logical step is to involve the school but I don't think that this is necessarily a school issue. Any advice?'

Talk about a new frontier. Neither of us had come across this dilemma before, and it is clearly a result of social media and a young girl's burgeoning sexuality. She had no idea posting intimate selfies would have such a huge implication. How can a parent protect their son or daughter from what another girl or boy naively does online? Though we believe, through our experience, it is rare that such an incident would occur, why risk a potentially dangerous follower of a student's 'open' account identifying the school from the uniform and prowling around the grounds? Ultimately, we advised the parent to speak to the head of pastoral care and explain what happened. However, the head of pastoral care could do nothing without a screenshot. If this is ever something you come across, and it concerns you, please take a screenshot as evidence. Only then can the person be talked to, cautioned, counselled or reprimanded more seriously.

Grooming

We cannot write about unwanted attention without referring to adults, often in positions of authority, who groom young people. These adults include teachers, celebrities, neighbours, priests, coaches, etc. Within the sphere of celebrity, arguably no one has shocked the world more with their history of rape and sexual assaults than Jimmy Savile. More than 500 victims have come forward to the police reporting Jimmy Savile and the NSPCC says his youngest victim was two years old. The children's charity believes Savile could be the worst sex offender in history. Most of his victims – 73 per cent – were children. In a rare public apology, the police admitted failing to build a case around the BBC celebrity who sexually assaulted people over six decades. The BBC, hospitals and others joined them in admitting to letting down his victims.

The story of Savile's mass sexual assault on the young, the handicapped, sick young men, women, boys and girls broke while we were shaping the content of The RAP Project. The horrible stories gave us impetus. Every student we address is familiar with Savile. Within the context of The RAP Project, we refer to his reckless disrespect of humanity and of the law as an example of why any victim of rape or sexual assault should come forward. If not, the perpetrator is likely to be a repeat offender and continue his or her criminal, destructive cycle.

Many of us have heard stories of the schoolteacher who has had sex with an underage student at one time or another. But the story of married teacher Jeremy Forrest who ran off with a vulnerable schoolgirl in East Sussex made quite an impact. The two embarked on a physical affair at his home one week after her fifteenth birthday. She had been a virgin. When the school and her family discovered the relationship, the two fled to France using fake names. Their escape across the Channel sparked an international manhunt. After eight days, police in Bordeaux arrested them at a bar. The Lewes Crown Court charged Forrest with abduction and having sex with the underage teen. Evidence surfaced that she was 14 when he began to groom her. So how as parents do we open up a discussion about these sensitive issues? Many of us listen to news on the radio while driving our kids to school, or while watching TV at home, and it's a good idea not to let the pretty harrowing stories about sexual assault that are so sadly often in the headlines go undiscussed. Our daughters also share with us their uncensored Snapchat news headlines, which can be graphic. Or, you can simply start a dialogue by using hypothetical examples about people in tricky circumstances and how they have they got out of them.

Teenagers can be particularly vulnerable to grooming. Issues such as exams, family life, pressure to be popular and body image are hitting our teens harder than ever. We need to be aware of our kids' emotional health. If we leave them to their own devices, locked in their rooms and online, we have no idea what they are doing, how they are feeling or what they are getting up to. Many parents, including ourselves, wish we had checked in with our kids and been more attentive to some behaviour issues that went unnoticed. If gone unchecked for too long, teenagers can get entangled in some complicated scenarios.

Deana knew a 10-year-old girl back in Brooklyn who went to her local Catholic church to make a confession, as she had done on several occasions. It was an open confessional where one sits facing the priest. She stoically made a list of her sins and received absolution. As she got up to leave, the priest grabbed her and pushed his mouth on to hers, kissing her fully. The little girl recoiled and ran outside. As that Catholic church was her Italian family's 'local', the girl had no choice but to return. Her parents never understood why she stopped going to confession.

Allison reported on a tragic story for Oprah Winfrey some years back. The story centred on an 11-year-old Belgian girl named Sarah Van Cleemput. Her father moved the family to northern California as he had been offered a fantastic job. An older neighbour, in the same business as Sarah's father, befriended the family. His name was Dick Stone. Within a few months, Stone had taken an intense interest in young Sarah. Her parents did not think it odd when he invited Sarah to his cabin in the countryside for some fishing and hiking. It turned out that he had been raping her for two to three years. Sarah had confided in friends, but begged them not to tell anyone what had occurred. At 14, Sarah wrapped her head with a towel and shot herself, hoping not to leave a mess for her family. In her wallet, she left a note that read 'Ask Dick'. A search of Stone's desk found a love note written to Sarah when she was just 12. The case was about to be dismissed for lack of evidence when actress Teri Hatcher of *Superman* and *Desperate Housewives* fame wrote to the prosecution team that Dick Stone had been her uncle, and had sexually molested her years ago from the age of five. Hatcher's subsequent interview solidified the case and the 64-year-old pleaded guilty to four counts of child molestation and received a 14-year prison sentence. Here are some signs, courtesy of Internetmatters.org, that could indicate your child is a victim of online grooming:

- Wanting to spend more and more time on the internet
- Possessing new items i.e. phones that you haven't given them, or tokens or presents that they won't say where they're from
- Being secretive about who they are talking to online and what sites they visit
- Switching screens when you approach the computer, or quickly shutting their laptop lid
- Using sexual language you wouldn't expect them to know
- Exhibiting reclusive or volatile behaviour

The story of a teacher drugging and sexually assaulting students at Southbank International School between 2009 and 2013 in central London remains unparalleled. Once a much-loved and well-respected teacher, William Vahey spent over four decades abusing young people on many international campuses. The discovery devastated the school, and The RAP Project has witnessed how many families still suffer anguish over the ordeal. Many of us remain speechless at the level of pain they have had to deal with. The trusted and married teacher would chaperone student trips abroad, drug male students, usually aged from 10 to 14, and then sexually molest and photograph them as they slept.

Vahey left Southbank International in 2013 for a school in Nicaragua called the American Nicaraguan School, and his crimes were only discovered there after a suspicious housekeeper stole a memory stick containing photographs of several nude boys, some being touched by Vahey. In early March 2014, the maid handed the USB drive to the school director Gloria Doll, who then fired Vahey. He committed suicide in a Minnesota hotel room later that month, after a warrant was issued to confiscate his computer.

Staying Safe Out and About

Citizens Report, a not-for-profit, independent organisation, aims to help residents improve the safety of their homes and streets. In its report taken within London's boroughs in 2012–13, Citizens Report found 11,376 reported knife crime offences. Weapons of any kind, whether real or just a threat, can escalate violence. When teens are confronted with a possibly volatile situation, particularly among young males, the best thing is to walk away or try to diffuse the situation verbally by lowering your voice and speaking very calmly. If someone attempts to take a phone, purse, watch, or other personal property, hand it over. It is just not worth risking one's life for.

A couple of years ago, as Deana was leaving her house for a RAP Project presentation outside of London, her mobile phone rang. The number that popped up was that of her middle daughter's school. Her daughter was 13 at the time. As we all know, getting a call in the middle of the day from your child's school is usually not good news. When she answered the phone, it was her daughter on the other end of the receiver. 'Are you okay?' Deana asked. Her daughter assured her that she was okay, but that she was with the police. You can only imagine the scenarios that went running through Deana's mind. Her daughter, who had been taking the London Underground to and from school since she was 11 years old, explained what happened next. As she and a couple of her friends were walking from the tube station to their school, they noticed a man following them. He proceeded to unbuckle his trousers and expose his penis. To Deana's total surprise, as she didn't have a clue that her teen even knew the expression, her daughter eloquently described the man as 'jerking off'. Her daughter and her friends stayed together while running quickly to their school and reported the incident immediately to the school receptionist. The police were then called to question the girls and take a description of the man, who had apparently paid visits to the school on previous occasions. To many of us, including Deana, this man wanking in the City of London at rush hour was bad enough. But when and where did her middle child learn the term 'jerking off'?!

As we mention earlier in this chapter, this sort of unwanted attention is not solicited and certainly not wanted, but it often begins when our kids start venturing out and travelling on their own. Deana's daughter and her friends did the right thing. They did not engage with the perpetrator in any way, be it through eye contact or conversation. They stayed together. They ran straight to trusted adults who were in a position of authority and reported the crime immediately.

Another story we have been told is of 15-year-old Daisy. The fastest route home for Daisy was a shortcut through an alley-way between her home and school. It was still light outside, so Daisy didn't think twice about saving time after a long day of classes, carrying a heavy backpack filled with books. She wore, as she did every day on her commute to and from school, her headphones. She enjoyed shutting out the world and listening to her favourite music. As she walked down the alley, someone suddenly grabbed her arm and she felt a dull object against her side. A young man was holding on to her. He said that he had a knife and ordered her to take him to where she lived. He threat-ened to hurt her if she didn't do as he asked. Daisy, petrified, thought if she obeyed him, he would let her go unharmed. She took him to the block of flats where she lived.

Once they entered her apartment, he grabbed her and groped her breasts and bum. Noises outside must have fright-ened him and, without warning, he fled her flat. Daisy never did see the weapon, so could not confirm if he was lying or not, but she immediately called her parents and in turn they called the police. The perpetrator was eventually caught doing the same thing to another victim nearby.

These are just two examples of many scenarios that teens tell us take place on a regular basis. Both young men and women can be vulnerable targets of predators. Whether it is the risk of having their phone nicked or having someone expose themselves sexually, there are tips that our teens (well, all of us actually) can follow to try to keep themselves safe. The motto for The RAP Project is 'Awareness is Power' and a con-scious awareness of one's surroundings is essential for staying safe. However, with so many of our kids walking around with headphones, the advice of paying attention is often falling on deaf ears.

Having been a criminal prosecutor, Deana keeps in mind the valuable advice shared with her by colleagues at the NYPD:

Know your whereabouts and what kind of neighbourhood you are in. Keep in mind that sometimes the most expensive, loveliest of neighbourhoods can be the most dangerous. People often assume knife crimes, sexual assaults and theft are far more likely to happen on council estates or in housing projects, where actually there are likely to be more police officers on patrol. But in wealthier neighbourhoods, where expensive cars, jewellery and watches are commonplace, people often let their guard down. The Metropolitan Police shares it reports and statistics online illustrating how crime rates vary from borough to borough. If you are interested, take a look at Crime Mapping and Crime Figures, both on the Metropolitan Police website.

Avoid wearing headphones unless sitting on a bus or on a train, and not when walking between two places. Walking while reading your smartphone is also not a good idea. Criminals are well-known for snatching phones and running, especially in busy shopping areas.

Remind your kids to **stick to well-lit paths**, and avoid cut throughs and alleys if they are isolated or rarely used at night. If they think that someone is following them, your child should cross the road, go into the nearest shop or walk to a bus stop or where there are other people present.

In addition to speaking about safety advice to our audiences, we also share what we have learned from our research with our own children. Deana has bought each of her three girls a 'personal safety alarm'. These alarms are small devices that can be hidden in the palm of one's hand, hooked onto a key ring or attached to a rucksack. There is a pin that is inserted into the alarm and, once removed, a deafening and piercing noise is unleashed. The aim is to frighten the attacker as well as to draw attention to a dangerous situation. But it is worth reminding teenagers that this is not a fail-safe safety device. The alarm does not negate the need for paying attention to one's environment and the safety tips we have already given. It does, however, provide an additional level of security, and is a safe option.

When we speak to young people, both male and female, we stress how important it is to avoid becoming isolated from others. Most of the crimes that Deana prosecuted occurred when a victim was on his or her own. If there are witnesses, a criminal is statistically far less likely to commit a crime. To illustrate this point in our presentations, we speak about a case that Deana prosecuted back in New York. A young man named Ben was riding the subway to work very early in the morning. He was the only person in the carriage when another well-dressed man climbed on and sat a few benches down. Ben, wearing headphones and deeply buried in a newspaper, noticed after some time that the fellow passenger was moving closer to him. He started to feel uncomfortable, but if he left the carriage, he would feel like a wimp and less of a man. True to his instinct that something was wrong, Ben soon found himself staring at the man's genitals as he had opened his zipper to expose himself behind Ben's paper. Men, whatever their age, have a complicated relationship with sexual aggression. Many describe feeling shame and deep embarrassment if they are hit on. We tell them not to blame themselves, and to allow themselves to feel vulnerable and frightened. Acknowledging fear does not make anyone less of a man.

Ben also ignored his gut instinct. This is something we urge young people not to do. The RAP Project encourages young people to follow their gut instincts because that little voice is usually speaking to them for a reason. Would the man have exposed himself if there were other people witnessing his behaviour? Probably not. So if our teens find themselves alone in a train carriage, we need to remind them to move to a busier carriage. If they are alone on a bus, they should sit as close as possible to the bus driver.

Closer to home, in 2013, a 20-year-old woman named Doris Chen stood up to a man who was sexually assaulting her on the London Underground. As she was commuting to work during the morning rush hour, she felt someone touching her bum. She then felt warm liquid streaming down the back of her leg. She quickly realised that the man behind her had ejaculated on her back. She courageously confronted her attacker and, with the help of another passenger, held on to him until staff from Transport for London and the British Transport Police arrived. The man was arrested and months later he was found guilty of one count of sexual assault, given a prison sentence, was mandated to participate in an intensive group therapy pro-gramme specifically for sex offenders and was placed on the sex offender register.

British Transport Police reported 1,399 sexual assaults on trains and stations throughout England, Wales and Scotland in 2014–15. In London, there is a now a coordinated effort to encourage people to come forward and acknowledge these inci-dents. Transport for London reports that 96 per cent of victims did not report sexual assaults or harassment that took place on public transport during 2013–14. As a result, the City of London Police, British Transport Police, the Metropolitan Police and Transport for London have launched a joint campaign called 'Report it to stop it'. The campaign's aim is to encourage passengers to report unwanted sexual advances and touching. The campaign released an effective video to accompany its launch. It shows a man and a woman on a train platform. They are both professionally dressed. The male actor is staring out the woman. She appears uncomfortable. They get on the same train carriage and his advances get more aggressive, culminating with him rubbing her bum. As his advances continue, the viewer is asked to evaluate, 'Would you report it?' The video makes the viewer question what behaviour they would tolerate and what they would not tolerate. After the woman is groped, she leaves the train and reports the crime to the police.

As the campaign launched recently, there is not yet clear evi-dence indicating whether more people are reporting unwanted sexual advances made against them on public transport. However, we feel very strongly at The RAP Project that teen-agers should feel empowered enough to stand up for themselves or for someone nearby and report any crime they witness. If your teen feels confident and safe enough, he or she might even take a photo of the perpetrator with their mobile phone as evidence. The link to the campaign can be found on page 47.

Young people share their stories with us after our talks. One 16-year-old at a local school said that it is not uncommon for her or her friends to be groped or brushed against inappropriately while riding the tube or bus. She said they accepted this 'as a matter of course'. When explained that unwanted touching of a sexual nature is a sexual assault, she denied this – 'They don't really count as sexual assaults. It isn't really a crime.' We asked her what she would do if instead of having her breasts groped, her handbag was stolen. Of course, she said, she would report the crime to the police. After discussing it further, and analysing why she felt differently about her handbag being stolen as opposed to her body being groped, she said, 'Well, I never had my handbag stolen, so I would be upset by it but I am used to getting groped.' We explained that no one should 'get used' to unwanted touching, and she should move away from the perpetrator and tell him or her the following: 'You are in my personal space and I need you to remove your hands at once.'

Attacks on women throughout several European cities on New Year's Eve 2015 left the world stunned. We will write more on international travel safety later in Chapter Eight (page 163), but it's important to touch on this here. An unprecedented number of sexual assaults, rape and robberies took place in Cologne, Frankfurt, Stuttgart, Düsseldorf, Hamburg, Helsinki, Zurich, Salzburg and elsewhere on 31 December 2015. Cologne, where there were over 500 reports of robbery and sexual assault, was by far the worst hit. Police there say some 1,000 people, mostly men, congregated at Cologne's central train station before breaking off into small groups that molested and robbed women. Victims were overwhelmed by the crowds of men and describe complete chaos with little apparent response from the authorities around Cologne station. Authorities are suggesting these attacks may possibly have been coordinated and committed by groups of about 1,000 men described by police as being of 'Arab or North African origin'. What does this mean for our teenagers? It means there are unforeseen threats on a scale we have not imagined previously. From reading reports, it is difficult to confirm if there were people trying to intervene and help the teenagers and young women who were being surrounded. We assume so, but we also imagine a large crowd of men would be very intimidating...

Dr Jackson Katz's 'bystander' theory, which we revisit in Chapter Nine (page 181), proposes that if one is witnessing unacceptable or criminal behaviour and being complacent, then one is subliminally giving the perpetrator the green light to continue his or her actions. The RAP Project agrees with Dr Katz, and we strongly suggest to our students the importance of taking a stand against antisocial behaviour. What do we mean by this? Here is an example.

In Camden, north London, an 18-year-old student went for a run. He saw a younger man, about 16, surrounded by two rather tough looking young men. He slowed down as he ran past, and listened to what was happening. 'Hey man, what time is it?' one of the intimidating men asked, as he pushed the 16-year-old gently. 'Nice watch. Can I have a look?' The young man looked terrified. He was definitely being mugged. The jogger felt he had to do something. So he stopped, turned around and approached the group of men. Suddenly, words poured from his mouth: 'Hi there! God, I haven't seen you guys in so long!' he said to the criminals. 'How is your mum? You really have changed!' This exuberant torrent took the would-be thieves by surprise. 'WTF are you talking about man? We don't know you!' They had been rumbled. If your child is younger, we would not suggest he or she step in and be a hero. We would ask them to call on an adult nearby, or a public official or if neither are evident, then call the police. It may be obvious, but remind your teenager or child to look to other adults for help if they are in a similar situation; or if they are witnessing a crime, they should seek help from an adult.

There is an interesting YouTube video called 'Social Experiment' that received a great deal of attention. The director wanted to see if commuters on a train would come to the aid of another passenger who is being sexually assaulted. There are two actors, a male and female, travelling on the same train carriage. The man starts to make unwanted sexual advances towards the woman. Despite her protests, he continues. A number of male commuters do intervene, a couple quite vigilantly. The theory is that if someone is called out for socially unacceptable behaviour and shamed by others, they will be less likely to repeat it. The link to this video is in the resource section at the end of this chapter.

Another thing we tell our teens during our sessions is to please pay attention when getting into minicabs. If their head is in their phone or if they are very tired, they may just climb into any car pulled to the side of the road. A friend recalled an incident involving her 14-year-old daughter. The mother booked a minicab to collect her much later after school, as she had drama rehearsal. When a black car pulled up to the school gates, the girl stepped in. She needed to head north and only 20 minutes later did she realise the cab was travelling south. Had she not been immersed in her Instagram account, she may well have noticed earlier that it was not her cab. Fortunately, it was a simple mistake and nothing more sinister. But it is wise to remind your child to identify themselves, confirm the destination, check the registration of the car and to be sure to only use registered minicab companies. It goes without saying that accepting a ride in an unlicensed minicab is a dangerous proposition. According to a recent report issued by the Metropolitan Police, there are approximately 200–250 cases of sexual assault claims made against unlicensed minicab drivers every year.

We tell our kids over and over again to always keep their phones charged and with them when out and about, keep their travel cards topped up, take their headphones off when in transit between cabs, trains, stations and home. We also recommend keeping some hidden cash tucked away somewhere that isn't their purse. We call this 'emergency funds'. One parent suggested keeping some money hidden in her home in case her teenagers needed it to pay a cab fare once safely home. At the end of the day parents can share personal safety advice that will hopefully reduce chances of someone becoming a victim of a crime, but we can never 100 per cent guarantee this. That said, why not talk to our teenagers about what's happening out there and share some of the things we have learned? Why not remind them to be aware of their surroundings, people's motives and remember to follow their gut instincts.

TRAVEL

Taxis: always use a licensed, recognisable minicab or taxi company

Remember to call home if you need to

Always be vigilant. Do not wear headphones

Visibility: walk on well-lit paths, do not take shortcuts or cut through alleyways

Emergency funds: have money on you in case you need to get home independently

Lifts: never get into a car with a stranger or someone who has been drinking

TOP TIPS

Remind your teen:

- Be aware of their surroundings
- Keep valuables hidden, including phones, cash, watches
- Don't take shortcuts or alleyways at night. Walk on well-lit streets and paths
- If they think they are being followed, cross the street and walk to a shop, bus stop or somewhere where there are other people present
- Carry a small personal alarm

- When travelling on trains, sit in a carriage where there are other people
- When travelling on a bus, try to sit as close as possible to the bus driver
- Walk away from a volatile situation
- Listen to their gut instinct. If they are feeling vulnerable remove themselves from the situation
- Don't get isolated. Stay where there are other people present

Resources

British Transport Police

www.btp.police.uk

Report it to stop it video

http://www.btp.police.uk/advice_and_information/how_we_tackle_crime/report_it_to_stop_it.aspx

Social Experiment

https://youtu.be/egeea61eafs

Transport for London: Staying Safe

https://tfl.gov.uk/travel-information/safety/

3 Digital Natives and Life Online

'The internet has been a boon and a curse for teenagers.'

J. K. Rowling

What do our teenagers do online? Now if ever there was a mammoth question! We began delivering E-safety presentations two years ago. Thanks to the five teenagers we have between us, we are in constant discussion (albeit often one-way) about what they are doing on their laptops and smartphones. Newspapers are filled with articles on body image, 'Like-spamming', cyberbullying, social media, Tinder, Grindr, gaming, grooming ... and now prime time TV features documentaries with titles such as *Revenge Porn* and *The Rich Kids of Instagram*. Despite there being no escape, this was never going to be an easy chapter to put on paper. But then we had an offline epiphany: we decided to simply distil the most important information we have gathered since starting this project three years ago and feed it back to parents with the intention of providing a resource of what teenagers are doing online, what the pitfalls are and what the laws are. We will also provide some personal online safety advice and share the best tips we have come across.

Ofcom, the UK's communications regulator, releases several studies a year on how Britons, young and old, consume TV, radio, Wi-Fi and other mediums. In 2015, Ofcom released a study finding that 12–15 year olds are spending twice as much time online as they did 10 years ago. That same year they found that young people aged between 16 and 24 spend more than 27 hours a week on the Internet. But how many hours a week do our teens spend on social media alone? First off, how do we define 'social media'? According to Merriam-Webster, it is a noun meaning, 'forms of electronic communication ... through which users create online communities to share information, ideas, personal messages, and other content (as videos)'. The RAP Project polled 3,000 students aged between 13 and 18 in 2016 and found that 11 is the magic number of hours they socialise online per week. This is outside of the time they spend on YouTube, watching movies, TV or researching online.

Young people who have grown up in the age of digital technology have been aptly dubbed 'digital natives'. How and why are our 'digital natives' going online more frequently than ever? Well, as the number of smartphones and tablets increases, so do the hours spent online. The mobile phone is now the primary device used for gaming according to Ofcom, and it reports that social media has tripled since 2007 with four in five social media users logging on to Facebook, Twitter, LinkedIn, Instagram or Tumblr at least once a day.

Ask yourself how many devices you have in your home and on your person that give you access to the Internet. When we ask members of our audience this question, many parents are often startled at the results. A YouGov survey conducted in March 2015 found the average British household owns 7.4 Internet devices, with smartphones being the most popular, and over half of British children have online access in their bedrooms without adult supervision. Many families have many more, and studies vary. Allison has 8 devices and Deana has 21. Yowza!

When Allison asked her 19-year-old son what teenagers did online, he quipped, 'Well, that's an easy one. We waste time.'

The amount of hours some of his friends spent playing online games, such as League of Legends*, despite a heavy academic workload, is countless. For those of you whose kids are doing this now, we can relate. With Allison's son now at uni, those hours, nights, days and weeks that he and his friends spent online bring back bad memories – the interactive gaming kept the younger kids (and parents) up with its loud laughter and online commands, and not one of the group of boys got enough sleep. Unsurprisingly, they could barely get up for school the next day and this later led to detentions, threatened expulsion and all sorts of trouble. The only positive, one mother noted at the time, was the fact that her son would make a great general, as he could certainly bark orders to his online comrades in arms! Perhaps an application to Sandhurst is in order? Or at least a future job as a middle manager...

To add to the joy and excitement of life online as a digital native, there is also something called *flamebaiting*, which some people do in jest or just because they want to elicit controversy and cause chaos online. According to Techopedia. com, 'Flamebait' is a message or post intended to arouse controversy. The flamebait can be introduced into any type of digital forum such as a social media platform, a comment thread or anywhere else that people interact online. So taking a position on a social situation, a teacher, a vote, a news story can all be an excuse to stir up some excitement or venom, or worse. Obviously Allison's son's line about wasting time being the number one activity online was made only in partial jest. The Internet as a learning and creative tool is one of the great wonders of the world. It has allowed our kids to keep in contact with their family and friends abroad,

---

* League of Legends (LoL) is a multiplayer online battle arena, real-time strategy video game developed and published by Riot Games. By July 2012, LoL was the most played PC game in North America and Europe in terms of the number of hours played – 27 million a day.

and our teenagers create PowerPoint/keynote presentations, produce music, edit videos and research information for everything from Computing and Coding to History, English and Geography homework. If they need to practise their Mandarin or French, learn to knit, understand Excel or make dinner, they just Google it. Remember card catalogues in your school library? Have you ever tried explaining our methods of research back in the day to your teens? No, neither have we. No point whatsoever.

If you need further convincing of our argument that the Internet is not a complete waste of time, take a look at what Ciara Judge, Konstantin Avdienko or Rob Greenfield have accomplished by using the Internet as a resource. They each describe how their one idea changed the world in their brilliant, inspiring TEDxTeen talks. Jack Andraka successfully researched and developed a test for the early detection of pancreatic cancer when he was only 15 years old. Really. Go on, Google it.

While there is legitimate time spent online, researching homework or composing music with GarageBand for instance, most teenagers aren't making medical or ecological discoveries. They are using the Internet to communicate and share their lives online. Facebook, Snapchat, Instagram and WhatsApp regularly top the charts in varying order of popularity. Despite the fact that you need to be a certain age to sign up for an account, Knowthenet.com found that over half of children (aged 10) polled ignore the age requirements and use social network sites anyway. The study showed that children first access YouTube at the age of 9; they use Internet slang and instant messaging at the age of 10; and at 11 begin their Internet activity in earnest. This is when they might post an image, a video or a negative comment online. Twitter and WhatsApp is used at the age of 12 and then at 13, the young teens try Snapchat, ASKfm and might send a sext for the first time.

Here is a quick breakdown of what these apps actually do:

Facebook

AGE REQUIREMENT: 13

Facebook is a social networking website that makes it easy for you to connect and share with your family and friends online. Originally designed for college students, Facebook was created in 2004 by Mark Zuckerberg. It is an extension of his short-lived 'Facemash', a website he designed to compare the attractiveness of two Harvard students, voting with the click of a mouse. Today, Facebook is the world's largest social network, with more than 1.5 billion users worldwide (Statista). Anyone with a valid email address over the age of 13 can join.

Instagram

AGE REQUIREMENT: 13

Instagram is a social networking app made for sharing photos and videos from a smartphone. Similar to Facebook or Twitter, everyone who creates an account has a profile and a news feed. Text messaging is also now an element. Users choose to have a public or private profile, and add followers by accepting or making requests. The filters provided to enhance photographs is very popular. According to Instagram CEO Kevin Systrom, Instagram has 500 million users worldwide.

WhatsApp

AGE REQUIREMENT: 16

WhatsApp is a messaging app that lets users text, chat and share media, including voice messages and video, with individuals or groups. WhatsApp relies on data to send messages, like iMessage or BBM, so it doesn't cut into your monthly text allowance. Statista reports that the service has 1 billion users worldwide.

Snapchat

AGE REQUIREMENT: 13

Snapchat is a video messaging application which allows users to take photos, record videos, add text and drawings, and send them to a controlled list of recipients. These sent photographs and videos are known as 'Snaps'. Users set a time limit for how long recipients can view their Snaps, from 1 to 10 seconds, after which Snapchat claims they will be deleted from the company's servers. However, recipients can capture stills by taking a screenshot before the Snap disappears. According to Statista there are 200 million users worldwide.

Twitter

AGE REQUIREMENT: 13

Twitter is an online social networking service that enables users to send and read short 140-character messages called 'tweets'. Registered users can read and post tweets, but those who are unregistered can only read them. Users access Twitter through the website interface, SMS or mobile device app. Twitter has more than 500 million users, out of which more than 332 million are active.

YouTube

AGE REQUIREMENT: 18, OR 13 WITH PARENTS' PERMISSION

YouTube is a video-sharing site created by three former PayPal employees in February 2005. In November 2006, it was bought by Google for US$1.65 billion. YouTube now operates as one of Google's subsidiaries. The site allows users to upload, view, rate, share and comment on videos. Available content includes video clips, TV clips, music videos, movie trailers and other content such as video blogging, short original videos and educational videos. YouTube has over 1 billion users.

YouTube videos have, for the first time, outranked TV in the 12–15-year-old category according to Ofcom's 'Children and Parents: Media Use and Attitudes Report'. The study found that 29 per cent of 12–15-year-olds chose YouTube videos as their top viewing choice as opposed to 25 per cent who chose TV. But what do they look at on YouTube? Well, it might be lip-syncing clips showing Emma Stone on *Jimmy Fallon*, a clip from a film, a music video or, in some cases, following their favourite YouTube stars or 'vloggers' (video bloggers). Our experience with teenagers and the subject of these vloggers varies greatly. Deana's youngest daughter Olivia is a mega fan of Tyler Oakley, a charismatic and cool YouTube star who speaks in support of the LGBTQ community. She finds his clips entertaining and inspiring. His following includes tens of thousands of kids who queue up to meet him in their onesies. Deana, to Allison's horror, twice took Olivia and a gaggle of gal pals to Tyler's book signings. She queued several hours at Arsenal Stadium for a selfie. What a saint!

In the UK, vlogging celebs PewDiePie, Zoella, Alfie Deyes, Tanya Burr, Tim Chapman, Niomi Smart, Dave and Phil, and Marcus Butler dominate the YouTube airwaves and command huge audiences. They share entertainment, comedy and life advice while being paid for subtly suggesting brands. In turn, they make millions.

Instagram can, rather alarmingly for our children's safety, reveal user's locations. Most importantly, however, Instagram gives users two options: private or public. One morning when Allison's daughter was 12, she mentioned casually that an Instagram user had asked her to enter a contest. Three competition requests followed:

1. Please send a photo of your hairdo.
2. Please send a photo of you wearing pyjamas.
3. Please send a photo for best swimsuit.

Fortunately, she intuitively knew this was suspicious. At the time, both were unaware of the private and public settings.

Now they are. But friends of friends can ask to join one's Instagram account, even if it is private. What teenagers tend to do is request to follow them so they can check out the person's account, photos and posts, and then decide.

One 13-year-old described an incident that occurred before understanding the importance of making her Instagram account private. She received a text saying, 'Hey.' The number then asked her name. She said it felt wrong and she ignored him. He then asked her for some 'nudes'. She ignored him but told a friend about him. The friend then followed him on Instagram to call him a creep. He then asked her for a naked picture. 'The whole thing was weird. My friend kind of bragged about it and I believe in a way she felt proud of his attention.' This illustrates the reality that young people, particularly young girls, seek approval and attention with regard to their appearance. What these girls need to understand is the possible ramifications when seeking and receiving this attention, which could prove sexually provocative. One thing we have learned about seeking attention by posting online from speaking to students is that it is far more a female issue and, surprisingly, the older girls are as vulnerable as the younger ones.

Setting Parental Controls

While many households enforce strict regulation on Wi-Fi access, others admit to feeling powerless over how many hours their children spend online. In reality, no matter how many controls you set in your home, you cannot monitor what your children may be exposed to when they are outside of your watchful eye. And, even then, images, videos and messages can filter through. We received a call from a friend who was quite upset when she found her 'innocent' and naive 13-year-old son on his iPod touch late one night looking at pornography. She had set all the controls and couldn't understand how these images filtered through or why he was even doing it.

Here's a guide to setting controls on the most popular social media sites:

Facebook

On the top right-hand corner of your home page, there is a padlock icon. Click on it and a drop-down menu will appear allowing you to control who sees your posts and whose posts you can see on your timeline. Additionally, it will allow you to block people and report abuse, pornographic or offensive behaviour.

YouTube

If you scroll down to the bottom of the YouTube home page, you will find an icon allowing you to regulate whether you want the videos restricted depending upon their content. If you turn the restriction mode 'on', videos with adult content will be blocked from being viewed.

You Tube   🔘 Language: English ▾   Country: Worldwide ▾   Restricted Mode: On ▾

Restricted Mode
- Restricted Mode hides videos that may contain inappropriate content flagged by users and other signals. No fi
- Your Restricted Mode setting will apply to this browser only.

🔘 On ⚪ Off
Lock Restricted Mode on this browser
Restricted Mode lock prevents others from changing the Restricted Mode settings on this browser.

Save

Instagram

Click on the lower profile icon on the bottom right side of your Instagram home page. That will allow you to 'edit your profile'. You will then see an icon allowing you to make your posts private by swiping to the right.

WhatsApp

To control who can communicate with you via WhatsApp, go into 'Settings', then go into 'Account'. In the account section, you can set your privacy settings. You can separately control who sees your profile picture and your status, and it will also allow you to block other people from communicating with you.

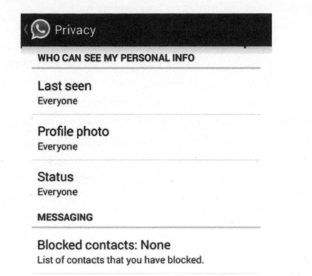

SnapChat

The ghost option appears on the top middle of your camera home screen: swipe up or press it. On the top right-hand corner there is a settings icon (it looks like a wheel). Press it and you will then be able to control who is allowed to see your Snaps and your story.

In terms of controlling your Internet at home, all of the major broadband companies – including Virgin Media, Sky, TalkTalk and BT – allow you to set parental controls. Normally there are filtering tools available to work across all home devices that are connected to your WiFi.

CEOP Command, the UK government's online criminal child protection agency, is a great resource for parents. They produce a website called Thinkuknow, which offers the latest information on the sites our teenagers visit. Thinkuknow advises parents and carers on what to look for when searching for an online security package that works for your family. They provide this helpful glossary of terms to help you manoeuvre through the labyrinth of choices:

- Filtering – content to restrict access to particular sites, such as pornographic websites
- Time limits – restrict the amount of time your child can be online, or set periods of time where your child can access certain sites
- Monitoring – where you are informed of certain sites that your child is attempting to gain access to
- Reporting – where you are provided with information about what sites your child has used

We as parents have experienced first hand what can happen when we don't pay attention to our digital native's lives online. Many kids today constantly check the number of likes they have on their Instagram or Facebook pages. Low numbers can affect self-esteem. Their addiction to online activity, to not wanting to miss out (known as Fear of Missing Out, or 'FOMO'), can affect sleep patterns and, in some instances, their mental health. Family time is often disrupted, family relationships suffer and our kids may isolate themselves behind closed doors. On the other hand, we have enjoyed more positive results by speaking to our younger children earlier on about the digital world. We aim to walk hand in hand with them on their social platforms. However, as this chapter illustrates, this is not a straightforward journey. Here are some hard truths:

- We cannot control what our children are exposed to online
- We cannot control what emails, texts, sexts or posts they receive via social media
- We cannot control the inappropriate pop-ups that occur when they are watching YouTube videos

But we *can* maintain a dialogue about their life online. You know how we ask our kids, 'What book are you reading?' or 'Have you seen any good films lately?' Now we can also ask, 'What's Emma been posting lately?' or 'Which of your friends' Instagram account is the most interesting?' This is the dinner conversation of modern families.

ONLINE

Only befriend people online you know already

Naked photos? It is illegal to send or receive them if you are under 18

'Likes' are not important; but who you are is

Incidents of online abuse should always be reported

Never share personal passwords or other details about yourself

Engage in a daily digital detox. Take an hour off

TOP TIPS

- Practise discretion online. No one needs to know your deepest, most private thoughts
- Online actions have consequences
- Pause before posting – remember there is no going back
- Befriend your kids' Facebook, Instagram and Twitter accounts
- Avoid sex talk online. Block anyone who makes you uncomfortable
- Don't flamebait or post angry statements inviting an escalation of emotions
- If you wouldn't do it face-to-face, don't do it online
- Avoid the 'iHunch', the forward curve of the upper back caused by constantly looking down at a smartphone or similar device

Resources

CEOP Command

www.ceop.police.uk
www.thinkuknow.co.uk

Internet Matters

www.internetmatters.org

KidSMART

www.kidsmart.org.uk

Ofcom

www.ofcom.org.uk

TEDxTeen

www.TEDxTeen.com

UK Safer Internet Centre

www.saferinternet.org.uk

Safe Online

https://www.theguardian.com/technology/2014/aug/11/
how-to-keep-kids-safe-online-children-advice

7

4 How Social Media is Influencing our Teens

Have you ever heard of 'Like-spamming'? Talk about a time-waster. This is when people on social media repeatedly ask for followers to 'Like' their post. For example, followers are urged to reach 200 Likes, then ask for 200 more. The teenagers we have spoken to are very open about how 'sad' this might appear but, despite this, admit to feeling insecure and vulnerable over a lack of 'Likes'. One sixth former told us, 'Logically, I know Likes don't matter. But if my friend has 100 Likes and I have 2, inevitably I feel badly about myself. I can't help it.' We hear the same sentiments from girls as young as 12 or 13. Imagine the time spent, wasted we would argue, spamming for Likes. Wouldn't it be better to read the Harry Potter books, learn to code or paint a Turner-inspired landscape? More about the 'Like' phenomenon later in the chapter when we discuss self-esteem (page 86).

Anyone with teenage children of either gender will recognise that social media heightens the insecurities of those competing online for the superficial attention that so many crave. One young woman who eschewed her number of 'Likes' for reality is 18-year-old Australian Essena O'Neill. The model attracted a huge number of Instagram followers with gorgeous, fashionable selfies surreptitiously endorsing brands on her news feed. Despite the fame and financial success, O'Neill woke up one morning and shut it all down. She explained to her fans that once she realised her work was vacuous and lacked meaning, she couldn't do it any more. Hoping to tell the truth behind the highly staged images, she admits she now despises the superficial nature of her previous job and is committed to writing about how she spent hours preparing for her online photos, with access to stylists, make-up and hair artists. In the end, Essena acknowledged that she promoted an impossibly high standard for young girls to aspire to. This resulted in them feeling 'less than'.

Back here in the UK, psychologist and fellow speaker at schools, Dr Aric Sigman, is highly critical of social networking. He believes it is actively displacing the time our teenagers spend socially interacting with real, as opposed to virtual, people. Allison heard him speak at her daughter's school and was specifically interested in his comments on the increasing activity called 'multi-screening', as well as the modern malady called 'screen addiction'. Using Facebook, the Internet and computer games while researching homework affects teenagers' cognitive skills, 'ability to pay attention' and 'concentration and literacy', according to Dr Sigman. He speaks with real concern on how fewer real life social interactions during key stages of physiological and social development is damaging our kids. 'Social media should be used as a tool, not a life,' he warns. He also said that it is different for those of us who have graduated into the professional world. 'Multitasking by switching attention between several screens may be necessary for adults at work, but is not what we should be cultivating in developing adolescents who should focus on the quality, as opposed to the quantity, of their information analyses i.e. their depth of analysis and concentration as opposed to breadth. This principle also applies to how they focus on people through social media.'

Furthermore, teenagers, and adults for that matter, admit to promoting a 'super positive' self online – 'Life is great!' or 'So happy to be here!' are frequent posts. In fact, the person might be feeling depressed or unwell. Without hearing someone's voice on the phone or seeing someone in person, it is impossible to really read what a friend or a family member is truly feeling in the virtual as opposed to the real world. We fear this is happening more frequently and the ability to intuitively sense real emotion is becoming less innate.

Another concern parents need to think about is the easy access to online pornography and the fact that our teenagers are both active participants by watching it and victims of a billion dollar industry trying to get them addicted. We speak about this in much more detail in the following chapter but with the surge in smartphones, young men and women have access to images and online videos 24/7. And, yes, a great number of young men are accessing pornography online. There are many studies that show that consuming too much online pornography can become addictive, hindering the opportunity for healthy, physical relationships with other men or women. For any parents who watch or who have watched porn, we think you will agree that the sex on screen is for the most part pretty hard core, with more pounding than foreplay and sensuality. In this case, we support offline rather than online lessons in love and affection through 'Friendship, Romance and Intimacy'. But, according to a BBC Newsbeat survey, in the world of virtually reality 25 per cent of teenagers are happier with online relationships than with their real life relationships.

Sexting

When we take The RAP Project to schools, it is quite common for staff to ask us to address the issue of sexting. What does it actually mean? Do our teens do it? Is there a legal age to do it? And what are the ramifications of doing it?

Sexting is the sending of sexually explicit photos, images, text messages or emails by using a mobile phone or other mobile device. According to an NSPCC/ChildLine survey, of

450 teenagers across the UK who participated, 40 per cent have admitted to creating a sexual image or video and a quarter of them have then sent it to someone else. In 58 per cent of those incidents, the image was sent to someone they were in a romantic relationship with. However, 30 per cent questioned admitted that they sent the image to someone they met online but had never met in person. In terms of receiving images, 53 per cent said that they had at one time received a sext from someone else, with 30 per cent having received one from a stranger. CEO of the NSPCC, Peter Wanless, has said, 'these results show that sexting is increasingly a feature of adolescent relationships', and is getting much more common.

So why is this occurring? There are a number of reasons and the NSPCC offers real insight into why teenage sexting is on the rise:

1. Not wanting to be seen as 'not sexy', 'frigid' or 'shy'
2. Pressure to sext as a way of 'proving' their sexuality
3. Feel harassed, threatened or blackmailed into sending pictures
4. Easier just to 'give in' to somebody who keeps asking for things
5. They 'owe' their boyfriend or girlfriend or are made to feel guilty if they don't send it
6. They are in love and trust them completely and feel like it's okay
7. They are in a long distance or online relationship with someone and want to have a sexual relationship with them
8. They feel proud of their body and want to share it with other people

It is crucial to point out that under the Sexual Offences Act 2003, it is illegal under UK law to take, hold or share 'indecent' images of persons under the age of 18. Teens always find this surprising and we understand why. When we point this out in our presentations, many students gasp or almost fall off their chairs in surprise. Yes, despite the fact that the age of consent is 16, the legal age to send a sexual photo, video or message is 18. Arguably here is an instance where law and technology have not quite reconciled, but regardless of the rationale behind it, if you break the law, there could be serious consequences.

Now, let's be frank. Some of you reading this may remember sending a sexy photo or receiving one decades ago. Back then, we may have swapped Polaroids. We explain to our audience that this is a luxury they cannot enjoy. Imagine a relationship ending and you agree to tear an intimate photo up ... well, they can't. In our experience, most cases of sexting begin in Year 8. For most 13-year-old girls and boys, they are beginning to think about sex and perhaps fantasise. It is healthy and normal. But sexting for our kids, through no fault of their own, is a hazardous practice. So we need to talk them through it: the ramifications, the law, but also the emotions attached to the desire to send a sexual message. We both support opening the dialogue in a matter of fact, casual way. For example, you might be making dinner with your girls and bring up an article you saw on sexting and revenge porn and gauge their reaction. This is a great opener, and while the girls lead the conversation, you can conclude it with the legal implications.

A study undertaken by the NSPCC and the University of Bristol found that England beats four other European countries when it comes to sexting rates, as almost half of our teen girls have sent sexual images. Not surprisingly, 51 per cent admitted to enjoying the thrill and did it to 'feel sexy or flirtatious'. Young men also participate, sharing photos of their manhood. In a RAP Project anonymous survey of 3,000 teenagers aged between 13 and 18, 36 per cent had received a sext. Less than 10 per cent admitted to sending one on.

We should add that we suspect these may have been under-reported for fear of getting into trouble, and that the percentages of students who do admit anonymously to sending these sexts on are clearly higher with older males. There are tables at the end of this book that illustrate the results of our survey.

To illustrate the perils of sexting there is an excellent video called 'Megan's Story' put out by the Australian government that we show to teens and parents at our presentations. It features a teenage girl leaving a school toilet, holding her phone and but-toning up her blouse. She sits down in the classroom and it is obvious that she has just sent a sexually explicit photo to a boy in the class. Within two minutes, the 'sext' has been circulated around the classroom, including to the teacher. These pictures can be sent around a class, a school or a group of schools very quickly. One student said, 'The worst bit is how the teacher got hold of it. I would never go back to school again.' The video is worth viewing and its link is at the end of this chapter. Young men may be slightly embarrassed, but, in our experience, are less traumatised if a naked photo of them is passed on and sent around the school or beyond. Young women, however, are much more likely to be horrified if an intimate image is shared with their boyfriend's mates or sent to other schools.

Not too long ago, The RAP Project addressed parents and teenagers aged between 13 and 18 at a school forum. During our discussion of sexting, a mum in the audience stood up and asked us to share what she was about to say with all future students and parents alike. She was a GP and on the admission board at a top UK medical school. Once her and her fellow admission colleagues narrow down their selected potential students, her department hires an IT consultant to thoroughly explore applicants' social media history. If they discover any images or posts that the board qualifies as unethical or morally questionable, it denies that stu-dent's application. Students might express outrage and ask, 'But doesn't that violate our privacy?' The answer, quite simply, is 'No'. Once you share something publicly, you relinquish your right to privacy. There is, however, a growing movement to allow young people the option to delete their Internet history when they turn 18. 'iRights' campaigners, including government officials and charitable organisations, are backing this initiative to protect our kids as they are growing up under the digital microscope. They claim that our young people should be able to live their online lives freely without the possibility of possible lifelong repercussions.

While in our day we might have been sent to the head's office for smoking or cutting class, now we see teenagers standing sheepishly outside their head's office, usually guilty of sexting. We came across a young woman who sold her images, which, when discovered, didn't go down well with her school administration. There is another case of a 15-year-old American girl selling nudes and videos of herself on the Internet and earning US$1,000 for making around 20 sales. She is now facing porn charges. There is an ongoing debate within UK schools on whether or not head teachers should involve the police if a sexting incident occurs. In September 2015, a 14-year-old boy sent a naked photograph of himself via Snapchat to a girl at his school in the north of England. Snapchat normally deletes direct messages within 10 seconds unless the recipient uses a screenshot to save it. The girl did, and shared it with a friend. While the teenager was not arrested, he was warned by police. The incident split opinion. One camp believes that young pupils are often clueless and irresponsible, and therefore do not deserve a criminal record. Others, however, fear there may be more to it and any sexting incidents should be reported.

Sharing indecent images has given rise to a phenomenon called 'revenge porn'. What is revenge porn? According to the Ministry of Justice, revenge porn is the sharing of private, sexual materials, either photos or videos, of another person, without their consent and with the purpose of causing embarrassment or distress. The offence applies both on and offline, and to images which are shared electronically or in a more traditional way, so it includes the uploading of images on the internet, sharing by text and e-mail, or showing someone a physical or electronic image. If convicted under this act, the defendant faces a possible jail term of up to two years and mandatory registration on the sex offender register. Queen Mary University of London is leading the way for advice on revenge porn. The law department has developed SPITE (Sharing and Publishing Images to Embarrass), a free legal advice service provided to anyone who has been a victim of revenge porn, or subjected to the 'sharing and publication of images to embarrass' by another individual. The link is in the resources section at the end of this chapter.

In November 2015, a 17-year-old boy was convicted under the revenge porn law for posting a video of his then 14-year-old girlfriend masturbating as an act of revenge for breaking up with him. Both of these young people's lives have been changed forever.

THE LAW OF SEXTING

- It's illegal to do so under the age of 18
- Think of the emotional and reputational damage it can cause
- Delete is not an option
- There may be severe and long-term consequences of impulsive actions
- Do not pass it on

If that is not enough for your teen to refrain from sexting or posting sexually explicit photos or messages, tell them to take what is known as the 'Granny Test'. Before they hit the send button, they should picture how their grandmother would react if she saw their photo or post. If Granny would blush with pride at their photo or post, by all means send it. However, if Granny would be mortified or suffer from heart failure as a result, we suggest they think twice. This test usually works.

Online Grooming

We have already mentioned the dangers of grooming in our chapter on unwanted attention, but it is worth going into the digital aspect of it in a little more detail here. Online grooming – a process by which an adult or an older teen establishes a relationship with a younger person via the Internet or social media for the sole purpose of pursuing a sexual relationship – is of growing concern. Paedophiles, or groomers, prey on their victims by trolling chat rooms and gaming sites popular with young people. Finding these sites is not difficult to do: both chat rooms and gaming sites have themes that make it easy to identify who will visit them. If it is a chat room talking about cheerleading, for example, there is a high likelihood that chat is going to be popular among teenage girls. Having said that, not all groomers are strangers to their victim – they may have met their victim at a social event or family function. Once a groomer establishes contact with a receptive and unsuspecting victim, their interaction becomes more direct and the relationship grows more intense over a period of time. This could be days, weeks or even months. As the online relationship develops, the groomer builds up a trusting, emotional relationship. In many instances, the groomer sends gifts or perhaps a mobile phone in order to speak directly to their victim without the knowledge of a parent or carer. Often, the groomer appears extremely intuitive to a young person's likes, vulnerabilities and concerns. To a vulnerable teen this person online seems to 'understand' them. In reality they have just done their research. As an experiment, why not Google your son or daughter's name and see what pops up. You might be surprised that there is information about them online.

Once trust is established, a groomer will steer their initially benign conversations and communications into more sexual ones, even requesting sexually provocative photos of their victim. By this time, the endless attention and compliments are addictive and the groomer moves in for the kill, so to speak. He or she suggests a face-to-face meeting. If the victim agrees to meet their groomer, despite the age of the person who turns up, the victim has already invested themselves emotionally in this relationship and is more likely to be taken advantage of sexually.

CEOP Command (formerly the Child Exploitation and Online Protection Centre) reports that 13–14-year-olds are the most vulnerable targets in these situations. Parents have shared with us examples of older men using fake identities as avatars during gaming. One 16-year-old boy grew so fond of his 'friend' online that the 'friend' flew from Lithuania to London for a visit. The parents by then had scuppered the groomer's plan but it took a couple of years for their son to come to terms with the situation. Another more recent and extreme case is that of 14-year-old Breck Bednar from Surrey who befriended an 18-year-old named Lewis Daynes through a popular gaming site. Their friendship grew over months until Daynes brutally sexually assaulted and murdered Bednar after luring him to his flat. Crown Prosecutor Jenny Hopkins said, 'He [Daynes] groomed Breck online using their shared interest in computer games and over a period of months he manipulated Breck, turning him against his family.'

So how often does this happen and how can we protect our kids from these online predators? The first question, unless it results in a viable crime, is more difficult as there is no quantifying data to establish how often this occurs. But what we do know is that our teens meet people in person whom they have initially only met online. According to the same BBC Newsbeat poll referred to in the previous chapter, of 1,015

15–18-year-olds surveyed, a third had met someone in person after originally meeting them via social media.

Deana does a particularly effective exercise with the teenagers in our presentations that seems to really hit home the importance of discretion online. Why share their most intimate details and photos with total strangers? She walks among the crowd, impersonating a nosy, pushy person on the street. She then asks each person she pokes with her finger questions including, 'Where do you live?', 'What school do you go to?', 'What do you like to do in your spare time?', 'What do you look like in a bikini?', 'In Calvins... ?' In every instance, each person recoils and looks at Deana strangely but immediately gets the point. The teenagers' body language is telling. Of course when it is put to them in this way, they would never disclose such information to a stranger. We then go on to explain that when they befriend someone or accept a follower on social media, they are doing the very same thing and this person would then have immediate access to their private world. In fact, it is far more dangerous disclosing personal information virtually because you have no idea who that person is. At least if someone came up to you, you can see them, judge them and then walk away. This they seem to understand.

Here are some signs to look out for if you suspect your son or daughter is involved in an inappropriate online relationship:

- If your teen becomes socially withdrawn
- If your teen's behaviour changes
- If your teen displays a heightened obsession with being online
- If they are adamant about the exact time(s) they need to be online
- If they change the screen when you walk into the room
- If they have received gifts, packages or a phone that you were not aware of them having

We also recommend speaking to your kids about what to look for in someone who might be grooming them with the aim of establishing an inappropriate relationship:

- If they are asked to keep their relationship secret
- If they are requested to communicate at odd hours
- If they are asked what they are wearing
- If the person is overly interested in their schedule or their family's schedule
- If the other person appears too intuitive about their life
- If the other person requests photographs of them
- If the other person often enquires as to how they feel about their parents and home life
- If they notice inconsistences in the other person's story i.e. age changes
- If the other person sends them gifts

Cyberbullying

This chapter would not be complete if we did not tackle the issue of cyberbullying. It is just what it sounds like: bullying online, via text or social media. ChildLine defines online bullying as 'when a person or a group of people uses the internet, email, online games or any other kind of digital technology to threaten, tease, upset or humiliate someone else'.

And just like sending a sext or advertising a house party on Facebook, these incidents tend to spiral out of control quickly. We frequently remind our audiences that they have it a hell of a lot harder than we did. In life offline as we knew it, bullying incidents usually ended at the school gates at the end of the school day. But today this is not the case. The harassment follows our kids home – on the bus, the tube, the walk home, during their homework and even to bed unless they turn off their devices. And many teenagers do not.

TEENAGERS AND SLEEP

Not surprisingly, teenagers are sleeping less today. One of the most comprehensive studies on technology and teen sleep deprivation was undertaken in Norway in 2015. The study polled 10,000 16–19-year-olds and found that the longer a teen spends using electronic devices, the worse their sleep will be. Doctors recommend teenagers get nine hours of sleep a night. Later screen time in the day influences the quality and quantity of sleep, with most teens polled admitting to getting five hours or less a night. The study, detailed in the *British Medical Journal*, strongly suggested that logging off is an essential step towards getting a proper night's sleep.

Staring at an illuminated screen before bedtime has been proven to hinder healthy sleeping habits. In 2015 the Wales Institute of Social & Economic Research, Data & Methods found that one in five secondary school pupils wake nightly to use social media. Can you imagine checking your phone in the middle of the night and reading highly abusive, critical messages? That experience coupled with the effects of not getting a good night's rest is not a healthy one. A study carried out by the Norwegian Directorate of Health analysed almost 10,000 older teens and analysed their usage of any device that had a screen, such as tablets, laptops, games consoles, smartphones, PCs and TVs. It found that those who used electronic devices in the hour before going to bed took longer to fall asleep. They were also more likely to feel they needed at least another two hours' sleep more than they actually got.

ChildLine, the children's counselling arm of the NSPCC, reported that more than 50,000 young people made contact in 2013–14 to say they were being (or suspected they were being) abused, either sexually, physically or emotionally, making abuse the fourth most common reason for contacting ChildLine. This is broken down as follows:

Physical Abuse: 18,769
Sexual Abuse and Online Sexual Abuse: 15,384
Emotional Abuse: 12,363
Neglect: 3,233

The charity also saw a sharp rise in the number of children suffering from cyberbullying:

- 4,500 young people talked to ChildLine about online bullying in 2015
- 50 per cent of young people have bullied another person; 30 per cent of whom do it at least once a week
- 43 per cent of young people have been bullied; 44 per cent of whom are bullied at least once a week
- 26 per cent said their weight was targeted; 21 per cent body shape; 18 per cent clothing; 14 per cent facial features; 9 per cent glasses; and 8 per cent hair colour
- 24 per cent have had a naked photo shared without their consent

Another difficult aspect of life online is the inevitable discussion about parties. It is much easier today to ascertain whether or not you have been invited to a party or a bar mitzvah or a dance than before. In the past, friends or acquaintances would host a party and chances are you would never hear about it if you weren't invited. Or if you did, you probably didn't think twice. Today, photographs and superlatives ('Best night EVER!') illustrate parties on line. One knows immediately if they have been left out. And while in normal circumstances, this might not really matter, once these events are made public on social media, one knows immediately if they were excluded. There is no new 'the invitation got lost in the mail?' It can be hurtful to know you were knowingly left out, and both of us have seen this first hand when our kids' moods suddenly head south when checking in online on Sundays.

We also need to discuss the not very nice phenomenon of 'fraping'. A frape is when someone hacks into someone else's Facebook account and then posts something highly inappropriate, rude or worse. A Year 10 boy who spoke to us after a presentation felt pretty bad about an incident that had recently occurred. He and a few of his mates went to a girl's house after school to hang out. She went downstairs when her mother called her and the guys in her room noticed she was logged on to her Facebook account. He described how the young men egged each other on and acted in a 'laddish' way. Finally one of them cracked, posed as the young woman and typed, 'I will suck anyone's dick for £10'. 'Well, when she discovered this, she freaked out. Her mother threw us out and the school got involved. We each had to report to the head independently and explain what happened. The guy who wrote the post was nearly expelled but in the end, only excluded. I won't be around fraping ever again as she was very upset. I felt really bad in the end.' This 15-year-old girl had her reputation damaged online. By deleting the post and reporting it to Facebook, some damage control was possible, but the incident still pains her today.

As social media becomes a larger part of our social interaction, parents can play a more active role in helping support our children when they feel bullied, excluded, or 'less than'. What are your kids doing online? Find out. Who are they following? Which of their contacts are most aggressive? Which are more prone to gossip? Ask them. Advise them. Help them negotiate the more complicated contacts in their lives, if they allow it. We don't advise pushing them, as they need to be independent and learn how to handle these issues, but we certainly can guide them. When we started doing this, there was a new trend that unsettled schoolteachers and deputy heads. If there was a problem at school, i.e. a bullying issue, those involved might text or call home and before the teachers could get wind of a situation, the parents would be ranting at them down the line. We call this 'Mama Dramas', and campaign strongly against it. Our kids, younger ones in particular, need support. But eventually, they need to mature and understand which battles are worth fighting, worth ignoring or worth reporting to a parent or teacher.

CYBERBULLYING TIPS

- Encourage your child to talk to someone they trust
- Keep copies of any abusive or threatening communications
- Do not reply to any messages received
- Block or cancel the accounts where bullying has occurred
- If persistent and severe, report to the school or police
- Take a screenshot if you need to report an offending sext

Body Image

Since founding The RAP Project in 2012, we have tried very hard to adapt to the changing needs of the PSHE teams and the students at schools. Initially, we focused on personal safety and helping teenagers keep safe physically. Then we realised they were grappling with less obvious safety issues as a result of their virtual lives and suffering from aspects of the media and its influences on body image. So it became apparent that it was equally important to keep them mentally and emotionally safe. Teachers working in pastoral care made similar observations and expressed the same concerns. The RAP Project owes credit to many academics for pushing us to add body image to our roster of presentations for their students. Traditionally, body image was considered a female problem and, to be honest, we rolled out our 'Altered, Airbrushed and Unrealistic' body image talk solely to young women. But it didn't take long to appreciate that young men are equally vulnerable. The number of teenagers unsatisfied with their looks and insecure about their physical shape is growing. Eating disorders are on the rise and there are unfortunately plenty of statistics to prove this. At one London school, a teacher described how she asked a room of 24 students to close their eyes and raise their hands if they were happy with their appearance. Only three students raised their hands. Quite sad, isn't it?

When we were young, we too had movie stars, fashion magazines and posters to contend with. Posters of Farrah Fawcett, Tom Selleck and Starsky and Hutch adorned our generation's walls. We strived to look attractive, but never perfect. Now, every TV show geared to teens features characters who are either absolutely gorgeous, super rich, vampires, wolves, or all of the above. They are impossible role models to emulate, but somehow set the bar for our teenagers. We explain to the students that with their studies, extracurricular activities, sports, etc. they do not have three extra hours a day to train like these actors do to achieve six-packs, thigh gaps and overall perfection. But Allison's daughter Isabel, despite total support for our work and being an intelligent 13-year-old editorial contributor, openly discusses her adoration of popular TV show *The Vampire Diaries*' lead character Damon Salvatore, played by Ian Somerhalder. Isabel is not alone in this, and nearly every schoolgirl agrees with her. The point is that, just like the beautiful, very tall, thin and perfect female models these young women are impossibly comparing themselves to, Damon Salvatore's physique is not easily achievable for their male counterparts. Isabel admits, 'I can't help it. He looks good.'

There were over 50,000 cosmetic procedures performed in the UK in 2013 according to The British Association of Aesthetic Plastic Surgeons (BAAPS). In 2014, the president of BAAPS, Michael Cadier, voiced concern over the number of young people seeking plastic surgery. Why is there a growing trend among young people to want to alter their appearance through cosmetic surgery? Celebrity plastic surgeon, Alex Karidis, attributes this behaviour to social media, stating 'for these girls, Instagram is a way of life. They want to document everything and want to look perfect while doing so'. For a lot of young people Kylie Jenner is, if not exactly a role model, then at least a person to emulate, or to aspire to look like. So when at 18 years old she explains to the *New York Times* how wonderful her plastic surgeon is for his lip-filler technique, these kids are going to be influenced.

Though the sexual expectations of watching pornography are discussed in the next chapter, we cannot talk about body image without touching on the influence of pornography. In today's pornland, women boast enormous breasts and are hairless save for the bouffants on their heads. Men swing around excessively large erect penises before aggressively slamming them into a passive young woman. These are role models and their sexuality is also influencing our teenagers. How can a young man not feel inferior when the average male porn actor's member is substantially larger than the average male Briton's? And the majority of female porn stars have had breast augmentation. As a result, most of our teenagers are defining beauty by less than realistic role models. The images they are inundated with are overtly sexual, airbrushed and often cosmetically enhanced.

Music videos, films, TV shows, adverts and selfies with filters to enhance reality all compete to support unrealistic body image. But we can remind our teenagers that all of these actors and models have had work done or are airbrushed. One of the aims of our body image presentation is to inspire students to take ownership of the images they are force-fed, interpret the subliminal meaning and then decide whether they buy into the message or products they are being sold. We ask them to please 'own the message' and not just 'buy it'. Sit with your teenager and scan the pages of a fashion magazine. Count how many images are sexual. How many illustrate a man or a woman as inanimate objects? We believe nearly all of the big name fashion brands, from Calvin Klein to American Apparel, have been guilty of this, and so many of us don't even notice it.

There is a variety of reaction from the audience when we pull up the infamous Dolce & Gabbana 'gang rape' advert from 2007 after our hard line porn section of the presentation:

- 'Hot'
- 'Gang rape'
- 'Disgusting'
- 'Male domination'
- 'Shiny'
- 'Voyeuristic'

The advertising industry is notorious for manipulating the public into thinking that if we buy a certain product we will look hot, get the guy, get the girl and enjoy unlimited riches and happiness. These are not new angles. But we find the advertising world is pushing the boundaries more and more. Is the proliferation of hard core porn influencing the advertising world and its media? We think so. The Dolce & Gabbana advert in question clearly promotes voyeurism, male domination, female submission and the message is quite honestly one of gang rape. In it, a young woman is presented pinned down by an oiled man with three men stood overlooking in the background. The effect is menacing, and they have even gone so far as to have the woman looking passive, weak and with a worryingly glazed look in her eyes.

It caused a storm on Twitter and throughout celebrity and fashion blogs at the time of its publication. It was quickly banned, but not before giving the designers endless publicity.

Our students, for the most part, are shocked at the image. Some of the young men maintain that it is sexy, and we explore this by eliciting reactions from the audience. 'Is this woman engaged with the man/men?' 'Are the men queuing?' 'Why is he holding her down?' We don't dictate whether they should love it or despise it, but we do suggest when flipping through magazines, books, music videos or porn, that they understand the underlying message and assess whether it is a healthy one for them or not.

International soap brand Dove has been exporting its message of positive self-esteem for over a decade. The company has made videos illustrating the extent to which Photoshop and computer image enhancing is used in advertisements. The point they are making is that our teenagers are trying to achieve a perfection that is not real. The Dove video we use in our presentations documents the transformation of a normal attractive woman into a plastic looking Barbie doll type character through digital alteration: https://www.youtube.com/watch?v=17j5QzF3kqE. After digitally altering her face by enlarging her eyes, reducing the size of her bum, elongating her arms and legs and whitening her skin, she is nearly unrecognisable from the original lovely woman. We show a similar video to the young men.

Eating disorders

How is this pressure manifesting itself? The number of teenagers admitted to hospital in the UK for an eating disorder has doubled from 2011 to 2014 according to the NHS. The NHS describes this disorder as 'an abnormal attitude towards food that causes someone to change their eating habits and behaviour'. And this is not an illness that just affects young women. According to Beat, the UK's leading charity devoted to supporting people struggling with this problem, 11 per cent of those suffering from an eating disorder are male. King's College London concluded in a 2013 study that 'about 4,610 girls aged 15–19 and 336 boys aged 15–19 develop a new eating disorder in the UK every year'.

Emmy Gilmour, the Founder and Clinical Director of The Recover Clinic, a London-based treatment programme for young women suffering from eating disorders, shares this: 'An anorexic weight has too long been presented by celebrities as "the norm" and young people wish to fit in more than anything else. They will then edit, crop and manipulate images to try to fit this mould as much as they possibly can. This starts an early onset of hatred to their "real bodies" or a motivation to starve, punish and manipulate their bodies to conform with what is a totally unrealistic goal.'

In addition to intense pressure from false 'perfection' online, there is also a proliferation of Pro-Ana (Anorexia), Pro-Mia (Bulimia) and Pro-ED (Eating Disorders) websites. University Campus Suffolk issued a report in 2012 entitled 'Virtually Anorexic – Where's the harm? A research study on the risks of pro-anorexia websites'. The study examined 126 Pro-Ana and Pro-ED sites, and warned 'that health professionals, educators and parents need to be aware of Pro-Anorexia sites and the risks they may pose'. Though many of these sites disguise themselves as a place where people can bond over losing weight together in a healthy way, the underlying agenda is to encourage and normalise eating disorders. There is no doubt that both young men and young women today consider appearance and body image a top concern. Let's look back at the RAP Survey, 2015–2016, where we canvassed 3,000 teens over a variety of issues. Remember the list at the beginning of the book? After Exams/School work, Body Image ranked Number Two in almost all age groups: Females 15–16; 13–14; Boys 13–14. Then third for young men aged 15–16. It is clearly a worry for younger teens, as the 17–18 year olds thought more about social life and sex lives.

If your teenagers are looking at any of these 'thinspirational' sites, speak to them about it. It may sound obvious, but tell them they look great. We constantly tell our audience and our own kids that if they eat healthily and exercise, they will look great! Be fit not fanatical. Let's remember that the skeletal actors and actresses are being paid to eat less. Amy Schumer famously admitted having to lose weight for her film *Train Wreck* and suffer hunger for several weeks. Julianne Moore gingerly walked up on stage at the Bafta Awards and exclaimed, 'I'm so hungry' to a wide audience as she accepted her Best Actress award for *Still Alice*. Is this normal? We don't think it should be.

If your teenagers are looking at any of these 'thinspirational' sites, speak to them about it.

CHARACTERISTICS OF PRO-ANA, PRO-MIA AND PRO-ED SITES

- Glamorise/idolise images of emaciated or very thin individuals
- Imply food and weight are the enemy
- Encourage and teach dangerous eating disorder behaviours
- Promote thinness at any cost
- Deny seriousness of illness
- Insist that eating disorders are choices, rather than an illness
- Attempt to mask toxicity by being exclusive and elite

Self-esteem

Almost everyone we address at schools is active on sites such as Facebook and Instagram, but the frantic self-promotion on social media is difficult for many of us to digest. When asked why they feel the need to be active on all these sites throughout the day, one young man explained it like this: 'We don't have a choice. If everyone is doing it, you have to, too. If you don't, everyone will think that you have no life.' Interesting, isn't it? By constantly posting images of their lives, our teens are in effect creating a life they want everyone to think they have. And the majority seek validation for it by measuring how many people 'Like' them on Facebook or 'follow' them on Instagram.

At a school recently, we asked a group of students how they would feel if they posted a photo of themselves and only received four 'Likes'. There was an audible collective gasp from the kids. One young man said, 'I would delete it right away.' When we asked why, he said, 'because I would think that people thought I was ugly'. We then asked the students whether they would walk into school tomorrow with a photograph of themselves pinned to their back asking people to put a tick next to it if they thought they looked attractive in the photo. In agreement, the students said, 'No way!' The reason they wouldn't do that, one young woman said, was, 'Because I wouldn't want to face the person who didn't "Like" me.' What our teens need to realise is that by finding self-worth in how many 'Likes' they receive, or don't receive, is setting themselves up for failure. A friend of ours recently reported that her very bright 16-year-old daughter seems more concerned with how many 'Likes' she gets on Facebook than on how many As she gets at GCSE.

Researchers at Brunel University London issued a report on the correlation between Facebook status and self-esteem. They found that 'people who received more likes and comments tend to experience the benefits of social inclusion whereas those who receive none feel ostracised'. Why would anyone seek constant approval from their peers and leave themselves exposed to meaningless criticism? Again, practising discretion is key. One 12-year-old girl told her 68 friends that she had broken up with her boyfriend via WhatsApp. Really? And is it vital for our kids to spam for Likes? Does anyone need to say someone looks fat in a post to 450 followers, including the named person?

We have written a great deal on how social media and the Internet can negatively affect our teenagers' self esteem and confidence. But of course it does also offer great support to those in need. As we will discuss later, teenage sexuality is extremely different to what it was in our era of teenage romance. Today's kids are far more open about their sexuality, and with their choices, and to this end the digital age seems to be quite a positive thing. YouTubers like Tyler Oakley, Ingrid Nilsen and Jazz Jennings celebrate their LGBT status. Their followers number in the millions. These millions include teens who are gay and straight. Tolerance and acceptance of peoples' sexual choices amongst our teens is very strong. When we first started working in schools, we were pleasantly surprised by how many students we met who were open about their sexual identity and confident in who they were. Needless to say, this is quite a change from what members of the LGBT community experienced in years past. There are countless blogs and websites offering online support to young people who are struggling with their sexuality, as well as offering an online community for them to reach out to. Websites like stonewall.org.uk has a whole area for young people who are struggling with coming out and who need support. This should come as a comfort to parents as we all want our children to be happy and supported, as reflected in the YouGov study published in March of 2015, citing that 88 per cent of adults polled would support their child if he or she was gay. Social Media and the Internet celebrate the LGBT community, making it more visible, and for that we should be very grateful.

We both now admit that we missed the boat for our older kids, now both 19. We were unaware how many hours they were spending online and what they were doing when online. We discovered the hard way and, as a result, now discuss in detail with our younger ones what they are up to online, what it means, how it is influencing them and when it is time for a digital detox. Deana likes to 'play dumb' with her kids. She asks her daughter questions as if she is completely clueless as to how to access certain social media apps. Her daughter proudly sits down with her using her own account and explains how it all works. This exercise gives Deana access to what is going on in her 13-year-old's virtual world without her even realising it. Experts recommend that parents start having discussions with their children about the Internet and social media from the age of 10 or 11. We recommend a family discussion on the subject, but of course each household will decide what is best for them. Nothing beats a debate and an exploration of specific websites and apps with our kids.

Through our research and speaking with educators, we have put together a list of helpful tips to encourage our teens to take a step back from their life as a digital native, and measure how the onslaught of social media, music videos, TV shows and beyond influence their self-esteem.

ESTEEM

Expect your body to change during adolescence

Selfies at breakfast? Slow down, phone down, get to school on time

Take stock. What makes you special?

Even if tempted, do not pass on a sext

Essential to 'like' on social media? Not really

Manage your sleep. You need eight hours a day minimum

TOP TIPS

- Take a deep breath
- Tune out social media for a period of time every day
- Practise discretion. Don't constantly post or respond to every message or comment
- Use the Granny Test!

- Beware of strangers bearing gifts
- Accept that there is no such thing as being or looking perfect
- Analyse how ads are manipulating you and how they make you feel about yourself
- Celebrate the 'perfect' you, whoever that may be!

Resources

Beat

www.b-eat.co.uk

CEOP Command

www.ceop.police.uk

ChildLine

www.childline.org.uk
0800 1111

Ditch the Label

www.ditchthelabel.org

Megan's Story

https://www.youtube.com/watch?v=DwKgg35YbC4

5 Pornography

'For the first time in history, children are growing up whose earliest sexual imprinting derives not from a living human being, or fantasies of their own ... the sexuality of children has begun to be shaped in response to cues that are no longer human ... they are being imprinted with a sexuality that is mass-produced, deliberately dehumanising and inhuman.'

Naomi Wolf, The Beauty Myth

One late afternoon last year, we received a phone call from the head of pastoral care at a secondary school. The teacher had invited us into the school on several occasions to address male and female students in Years 10 and 11. She was concerned about a young girl, a very young girl in fact, who she feared was involved in an unhealthy relationship with one of her peers at school. The 13-year-old girl in Year 8 was showing signs of emotional distress, and her body shape was also changing very rapidly. She appeared to be obsessed with her appearance, which she admitted wasn't that unusual for a girl of her age. However, something else was occurring as well. She observed a rapid transition from a calm, self-confident girl to an insecure and unhappy one, and this, coupled with the other observations, immediately raised alarm bells. After some initial talks and gentle persuasion, young Katie began to show signs of trust and opened up about what was going on.

Katie had been 'seeing' Ethan since they were in Year 6. They grew up on the same street, enjoyed each other's company and one day he reached to hold her hand. It felt perfectly natural for her to accept it. Then, in Year 7, he asked to kiss her. Their friendship at that point showed all the signs of a sweet and innocent romance. The teacher knew Ethan as well, as he was also one of her students. He was a lovely young man and was always very respectful.

Suddenly in Year 8, however, Ethan started to change. He had two older brothers, one in Sixth form and one in Year 11. He watched porn with his big brothers and then began to show Katie what he had been viewing on line. Katie explained to her teacher that she found it 'gross' and 'disgusting' at first, but found Ethan getting very excited about it. He began moving at a faster pace, requesting heavier make out sessions and moving his hands onto her breasts. He became more sexually charged, and more demanding. She really liked Ethan, but found her new sexually aggressive boyfriend intimidating – although not enough for her to break up with him. 'What would my friends and family say?' she thought.

Katie then described a worrying incident, one that even shocked the experienced head of pastoral care. She was surprised to learn from Katie about Ethan's transformation from a shy young suitor to someone so aggressive. Ethan wanted to watch porn with Katie, and he showed her a video showing an intense oral sex act. The video portrayed a young porn actress forced to take the man's penis deep into her mouth quickly and forcefully. Ethan then asked Katie to try it, and she did. She was sick. The following week, he asked to watch another video. As she didn't want to lose his friendship, she agreed to it. This time he showed her an anal sex act between a man and woman. That was it, Katie thought, and left his room and house for the last time. Her relationship with Ethan, which had started out so innocently and tenderly, had quickly transformed into something very different.

The teacher had contacted us to see if we could offer any advice. While we have spoken to girls in Years 7 and 8 about some sexual issues, this seemed an extreme situation to us given their age. We suggested she talk to the family about getting Katie to a therapist for several sessions. While Katie had consented to Ethan's requests, neither of the young teenagers had the maturity to consider the porn videos, the acts, their implications and the aftermath.

With time, family support and therapy, Katie came through this period in her life. She is no longer friends with Ethan as later in the academic year he and his family moved away. Katie is not the only one who needed therapy as a result of this situation –we would advise that Ethan does too. The head of pastoral care feels for Ethan as well, and we agree. Young men are victims of pornography, and are watching hardcore videos at record rates. He was a 'victim' of over-exposure to hardcore porn.

We incorporated a discussion on pornography into The RAP Project primarily because the young women in our audience told us in no uncertain terms that we had no choice but to bring the message to the boys. As we began our research we were immediately struck by some pretty startling statistics. Here's a short True or False quiz for you:

TRUE OR FALSE

- Teenage boys are the largest consumers of online pornography
- The average age a person in the UK first comes across online porn is 11 years old
- Seven out of ten 18-year-olds say 'pornography can have a damaging impact on young people's views of sex or relationships'

If you answered 'True' to all of the above, you were right. If you got one or two wrong, you may need to take a closer look at what your teenagers are up to. But you are not alone, as it is a very difficult subject for many parents to get their heads around. Five years ago, when a trusted middle-aged male friend suggested to Allison that her then 13-year-old son was 'most definitely looking at porn', she dismissed this as 'impossible'. Deep in denial, she could not fathom her 'little' boy looking at sordid, carnal activity online. But the truth is, he may well have been. Not because he was disturbed or perverted but because the practice of watching porn is an extremely popular one for teenage boys. The RAP Project surveyed over 3,000 teenagers aged between 13 and 18, and the average percentage of young men who admitted to watching porn online was 82 per cent. In contrast, 20 per cent of young women admitted to watching it. Porn is undeniably a popular pastime. And, as we have discovered through numerous presentations, very few parents have discussed porn with their teenagers.

When Allison did broach the topic with her son when he was 17, it was too late. Here's what happened ... While having dinner with her son, Allison nonchalantly posed the dreaded question – 'Mike, do you watch porn?' Mike nearly choked on his bolognaise and looked at her in utter shock. He left the table and headed upstairs. 'Where are you going?' Allison asked. 'I've got chemistry homework, Mike replied. 'But chemistry is not one of your A level subjects.' 'Exactly.' Door slams.

The RAP Project strongly promotes discussing pornography with your children. You do not need to get into too much detail – it will be embarrassing enough for them, perhaps you as well – but we do feel the need to clarify that sex in these videos has very little to do with real life intimacy; there is no kissing, hugging or sensuality. We ask the young men and women at every RAP presentation if they have ever spoken to either or both of their parents, at least one of them, about porn. Slowly, one, two, three hands gingerly go into the air. At best, we have seen 10 teens put their hands up. If we consider that most of our audiences number between 100 and 200, this is pretty shocking. It measures 5–10 per cent overall. Yes, it is awkward. But, as *Psychologies* magazine reports, teenage boys aged 12–17 are the largest consumers of online porn in the USA and the UK, so how can we ignore the fact that porn is influencing a generation of young people about sex? Is this something we really want to ignore? Early sexual experiences and romantic relationships are the building blocks of future relationships. Don't we want our children to be as healthy as possible? According to a study in *Psychologies*, pornography is a no go area for 75 per cent of parents who avoid discussing it with their teenagers. Whatever statistic we look at, communication on pornography is low. Fortunately, there is a momentum to counter this, and experts are suggesting we start talking about online porn to children as young as 10 years old.

After we ask the students if they have ever spoken to their parents about this somewhat awkward subject, Allison asks if anyone would be brave enough to describe the conversation. Here's what some of them have to say:

'My dad told me not to ram women like they do in porn ... that women don't like it that hard.' (Year 11 boy)

'My mum told me that women in porn videos do not have realistic bodies and warned me against comparing my body to those in the videos. She also said not to let boys make me feel insecure if I didn't look like a porn star.' (Year 10 girl)

'Dad told me that real men don't watch porn. They have confidence with women and know how to take care of them.' (Year 12 boy)

'It was probably the most excruciating moment of my life. My mum started speaking loudly about porn at McDonald's. The whole restaurant must have heard this. "So, I have been looking at your browsing history and I have some questions about what you are looking at." "Uhhh, Mum, I was just curious that's all. Don't worry I rarely look at it." She replied, "Good. I don't want you watching porn EVER." I nearly choked on my chips.' (Year 11 boy)

Speaking at the Sunday Times Festival of Education in 2015 we met a woman who teaches sex education at schools around the country. Claire Kennedy described to us how she would open up a sex education session with 15-year-olds. Having asked her students to make a list of words or phrases that they would freely exchange with 'having sex' or 'making love', she would write them on the board. 'Nailed', 'hammered', 'screwed', 'pummelled', 'laid' led the list. We were gobsmacked. Claire said, 'You'd think we were opening a DIY store.' This is not the lingo of love.

Hard-core pornography is changing the way young people perceive sex. The concept of very natural, human erotica is not what it used to be. Log on to free porn websites today and you won't find two people making love on top of a bonnet of a car or having sex in a candlelit bedroom. In the seventies we may have surreptitiously looked at our father's *Playboy* and *Penthouse* magazines. We saw what seemed at the time shockingly bold photographs of curvy, naked women alongside smutty stories. These centrefolds did objectify women, but in an era of women's lib many of us couldn't help but notice these women were proud of their bodies and were well paid to show them off. But the magazines were off limits to us for a reason, and getting caught was highly embarrassing. Today, in comparison to modern porn and its content, these nude shots are frighteningly innocent. The most controversial photo of its time was *Hustler* magazine's infamous meat grinder shot published in 1978, depicting a woman's legs sticking out of a barbaric cold metal kitchen utensil, her brain and heart reduced to a pile of mincemeat. Publisher Larry Flint had gone 'hard core'. But now these images of 'hard-core' pornography pale in comparison to what is accessible to teenagers in the twenty-first century.

Academic Gail Dines, author of *Pornland: How Porn Has Hijacked Our Sexuality*, is a harsh critic of porn and believes that it perpetuates a harmful culture for today's young people. She explains: 'The question I pose in *Pornland* is, what does it mean to grow up in a society where the average age of first viewing porn is 11 for boys, and where girls are being inundated with images of themselves as wannabe porn stars? How does a boy develop his sexual identity when porn is often his first introduction into sex? What does it mean for a girl or young woman to see herself as a desired object rather than a desiring subject? What do sexual relationships look like when sexual identity is constructed within this porn culture?' While developing our talks on porn to teenagers, we call on Dines's work. We know our kids are looking at some deviant, misogynistic visuals online and we agree with her when she says, 'To think that men and women can walk away from the images they consume makes no sense in light of what we know about how images shape our sense of reality.'

Here's a story that some of you may find familiar. A mother we know went in to say goodnight to her 11-year-old son. The boy, shy and reserved by nature, was tucked under his tent-like duvet watching a video on his iPod touch. Startled, as she thought he would be reading or asleep, she took the device and found some disturbing images within a porn video. Why had the parental controls she and her husband had so painstakingly put in place failed? How had hard-core porn filtered through their Internet security wall? Then, her inner dialogue swerved from anger and blame to admission. Thinking back, she realised she had never actually spoken to him about pornography and sex. She spoke to Deana about this, who suggested he was probably going to come across these images with friends or at school anyway, adding that no matter how many parental controls you set up, the majority of boys are going to watch porn. We can't 'control' everything that our children are exposed to inside or outside of the house. And we know that it is a subject that many parents have trouble talking to their kids about, especially for the young boys who would rather die than sit down with mum or dad over a cup of tea to discuss the content of their favourite porn sites. We know that by nature most parents find this subject matter difficult for a variety of reasons, but we believe the time for shame and denial is over, and the sooner we speak to our kids about it, the better. First we need to understand to what they are being exposed, how the images are affecting their expectations and self-esteem, and then have the conversation.

In 2016, Dr Miranda Horvath, co-authored a report entitled, '"Basically … porn is everywhere" A Rapid Evidence Assessment on the Effect that Access and Exposure to Pornography has on Children and Young People'. The report found that pornography influences attitudes towards sex and relationships and could lead to young people having sex at an earlier age. The Children's Commissioner and Middlesex University concluded, 'a significant number of children access pornography'. Horvath, a senior lecturer in psychology, defines porn as, 'full of explicit shots of sexual acts and genitalia'. Students, teachers and parents often ask us if we think the proliferation of porn impacts the behaviour of sexually active teenagers. The fact is, throughout our own research and as Dr Horvath writes in the report, there is very little hard evidence actually supporting this. What we do know when we bring The RAP Project to schools is that many students of both sexes readily admit to being influenced by porn, in different ways. Young men and women talk about the stress of body image, and girls in particular explain they do not want to perform some of the things that boys are requesting, having watched it online. Dr Horvath's report also concludes, not too surprisingly, that boys and young men are more likely to watch porn than their female counterparts. The motivations have not changed between generations: curiosity, pleasure and peer pressure.

It is no secret that porn is readily available on and off line, and that, in recent years, the most common way to access porn is via the Internet. This makes it very hard for adults to moderate what kids are looking at and, in some cases, distributing. So many teenagers have smartphones, 24/7 access to online photographs and videos, so our kids can go online and type in 'free porn' or 'porn hub' at any time. Looking back, it is hard to remember the transition from monitoring what we allowed our children to watch on TV, to what they downloaded on the family PC, to what is happening now. We can't speak for all of you but we can say that we remember giving our children a laptop for Christmas or a birthday. We acquiesced to their pleading: 'We need laptops for school. We have so much research to do.' And they do. Students today, from Year 7 onwards, have quite a workload to plough through for school. But within a blink of an eye, our kids were in their bedrooms and online. Yes, doing homework, but what else? The reality is, it is never too late to discuss these awkward subjects. Why? Because our teenagers are watching porn! Or will at some point. Keep in mind the conversation may be more of a monologue, as our kids may be too embarrassed to open up, but shouldn't we find out what it is that is keeping them so entertained?

The following is how we broach the subject of pornography with our students. We open the section with the following: 'We support healthy relationships between all sexes, straight, gay or bisexual. One's sexuality is a private, personal matter. Erotica is healthy and part of our human condition. And there may even be some scope for porn; it is not for us to judge. But we are critical of hard-core pornography that promotes rape culture and misogyny. We promote an age-old formula – "Friendship, Romance, Intimacy" – for building healthy relationships. But we fear hard-core porn is preventing these building blocks from forming a solid foundation.'

We often hear sighs of relief and a little bit of laughter, especially when Allison describes watching porn online … for her job. But the first slide puts things into perspective:

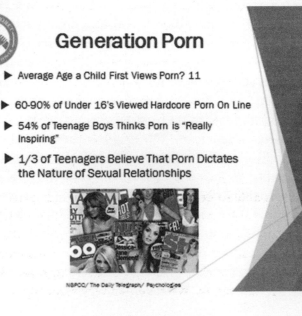

Generation Porn

▶ Average Age a Child First Views Porn? 11

▶ 60-90% of Under 16's Viewed Hardcore Porn On Line

▶ 54% of Teenage Boys Thinks Porn is "Really Inspiring"

▶ 1/3 of Teenagers Believe That Porn Dictates the Nature of Sexual Relationships

NSPCC/ The Daily Telegraph/ Psychologies

Herein lies the dilemma: erotica and pornography are as old as humankind. It is inevitable that hormonally charged teenagers will want to take a look at some erotic visuals of people having sex. But the visuals now are more likely to depict unrealistic body types and promote misogynistic storylines. Maybe we see three men and a woman having sex, and she is crying in pain, not pleasure, or a couple on the sofa, where the woman's T-shirt reads, 'Dumb Slag'. The tag lines of many of the videos include the following words: 'Gag Me', 'Bitch', 'Stepdaddy', 'Dominate'. We explain how this makes us angry and ask the audience, 'How can this promote healthy relationships? Remember "Friendship, Romance, Intimacy"? Where is that represented in porn? And, believe us, sex is much more satisfying when you can enjoy a close, intimate relationship.'

At this point, the students are paying very close attention. The boys, often quite diffident at the start of the presentation, are the first to ask questions: 'Why do you think porn is getting more hard-core?' Before we share our opinion, teachers often speak up to share theirs. One teacher at a grammar school blamed the advent of smartphones and endless access to porn websites. Inevitably, there is discussion and agreement on how these themes are filtering down to storylines in TV, film, adverts and, let us not forget, music videos. Another sixth form head at a state school in north London said that, 'Boundaries are continually being pushed and more and more shocking images are required to elicit a reaction. The visuals have to be more and more illicit to elicit a response.'

In worst case scenarios, some of the hard-core pornography trivialises rape. With Deana's background as a sex crimes prosecutor, she is able to detail cases about rape and sexual assault first hand. There is nothing trivial in her retelling of what her victims endured and have to live with for the rest of their lives. Having spoken at over 100 schools, female students more often than not ask us to address the serious nature of rape jokes and how they are not funny. We take this very seriously and make the point loud and clear by defining the legal meaning of rape and explaining how it is a violent and controlling crime which deeply affects the victim physically, emotionally and socially for years to come.

Teenagers tell us that many find porn educational. 'No,' we tell them. 'Porn is not educational.' The teenage boys often laugh when we ask them if they learn how to drive by watching the action film *Need for Speed*. There is no intimacy, touching, caressing or kissing in porn, but in most cases, there are oversized breasts, tiny waists, Kardashian-style bums and an aversion to pubic hair. In a study by The Institute for Policy Research in August 2014, 8 out of 10 young women (77 per cent) said that, 'pornography has led to pressure on girls or young women to look a certain way'. Almost as many (75 per cent) say, 'pornography has led to pressure on girls and young women to act a certain way'.

> 'You have got to talk to the boys about porn. Tell them we do not have the kind of bodies they see online. We don't want to do some of the things those actresses do. They pressure us and we don't like it. It makes us feel insecure.'
> (Year 12 girl)

When we first began speaking at schools to teenage girls only in 2012, they were adamant: 'You have to bring your presentations to the boys,' they begged. These young women were angry, insistent and, notably, vulnerable. Expectations are distorted, according to the girls. 'I don't feel comfortable with "anal"', we have been told. 'Anal' is now short for anal sex, which in our opinion, is quite a sophisticated and mature physical act. 'If you are mature enough to be intimate with someone, then we think you should be mature enough to talk about what you feel comfortable doing with someone sexually,' we say. The media attention showered upon anal sex in recent years is notable. Pick up a copy of

Marie Claire, Cosmopolitan or log on to *Slate* magazine, and you are likely to see a mention. The explosion of interest in the rather sophisticated sexual act is often linked to the proliferation of its popularity in porn. Indiana University conducted a survey in 2010 which was published in *The Journal of Sexual Medicine* that same year. The survey showed that there was an increase in anal sex from 16 per cent in 1992 to 40 per cent in 2010. We cannot help but think that this increase runs parallel with the central themes of pornography today: domination and subjugation over women. Anal sex is a private choice, an intimate act, but is it something that our 16-year-old daughters should be expected to participate in?

We regularly speak to teenagers about these issues of porn, body image and sexual expectations, and here is what some 17-year-old boys shared with us:

Q: Is porn part of everyday culture?
A: Porn is part of a private culture. It is a very private matter and watched alone and not talked about with other people.
A: The boys who talk about it are either immoral or immature.

Q: When did you first start watching porn?
A: 13.

Q: Do girls you know look at porn?
A: It is very rare for girls to look at porn. There is one girl I know at school who says she loves it. She is a scary animal.

Q: What do you look for in porn?
A: Well, the regular stuff, on Porn Hub. Sex. For some really deviant stuff, shock factor and for a laugh, maybe we look at Japanese porn. There is some very sick stuff out there, one video involves a teenage girl and an octopus. It is sick. Or sites that show orgies. Just for fun, not erotic stuff.

Q: Do you think porn today influences relationships?
A: It depends on the guy. If he has morals, no. The problem is, for us boys, whatever you say, you're a rapist. We are always the bad ones. We are just blamed for everything. Girls can be teases. One minute they are all over you and the next, brutal, BAM ... you don't exist.

Q: Have you ever been in a relationship for more than a month?
A: No. Never. We have such heavy workloads, there are so many people in the world. Many of us are afraid of commitment. You have to deal with social media, literally 'spiderwebs' of gossip and lies. It just isn't worth it.

Q: Are hook-ups easier?
A: Hook-ups are much more popular because it is so much easier. You literally have a shower, comb your hair and show up.

A: Every girl we know is insecure.
Q: In what way?
A: Their body image, intellectual abilities, popularity. It is crazy. And then on top of that, they turn on each other. It's just shitty.

And here's what some girls of the same age had to say. Beware, it is pretty eye-opening stuff:

Q: When did you first come across online porn?
A: I was really young, about 10. One of my friends showed me a naked man. I was fascinated.

Q: Is porn very important to your generation?
A: Definitely. The standards, expectations. Boys love to talk about how often they masturbate, different porn categories. It is not very pleasant.

Q: Why do you watch it?
A: Well, if you want to learn how to bake a cake, you Google it. I wanted to learn to be a better lover, so I approached it in the same way.

Q: Do you feel pressure to look a certain way? Do certain things?
A: Yes. Anal sex. Deep blow jobs. It is awful.
A: Guys want us to look stick thin, with big boobs and childlike vaginas.
A: Girls are so insecure. We are being completely exploited, viewed as objects in dominant, submissive positions. And then we are told to change with new skin, diets, make-up. And when you reach 13, 14 you are obsessed with how many Likes you have online. The pressure is intense.

Q: And what about body image?
A: Apart from the tiny frame and oversized breasts being the ultimate body type, impossible to achieve, guys also like us to dress up. Ann Summers is a big thing. I remember when I was 16, my then boyfriend and I went in to the store. He chose crotchless underwear and bras without nipple coverage. He then looked through the peephole and watched me model these. I remember feeling like the underage girls in the film *Taken* who were on sale to various older men.

Yikes. These stories are pretty shocking to us. Some of these teenagers are so highly sexualised at such a young age, but do they know what they are doing? Are they enjoying it? Are our daughters comfortable doing these things? If not, then why are they doing them? Some of the above scenarios are racy for adult fare, let alone for 16-year-olds. Where is the room for an emotionally mature physical relationship in all of this? Teenagers are easily influenced, and young women can also pressure their counterparts. Aren't romantic relationships in the teenage years difficult enough to navigate? Our kids have so much pressure to contend with: academics, appearance, popularity, etc., but the added dimension of social media brings even more emotional strain, distorting and influencing attitudes.

After one particular article published in *The Times* about The Rap Project's work with boys and porn, we received some interesting feedback from two former porn addicts:

Dear Allison and Deana,

I recently read the article in the Times 2 newspaper concerning your educational program for young boys on the subjects of sexuality, sexting, consent, and most importantly Internet porn. I am a member of the first generation to grow up with home Internet access, and I was a consistent porn user from age 9 to 24 (I'm 25 now). You two are absolutely right that children's and teens' easy access to porn is a problem. It wasn't until a year ago that I realised just how much using porn had damaged my life, my relationships, and my self-respect, and I vowed never to use it again ... I was a porn addict. Even though I considered my use normal and within reasonable limits, I can see now that I was addicted all throughout my adolescence and into adulthood. Like any addict, I used my behavior of choice to escape from difficult emotions. Even shame about using porn itself drives addicts back to porn in order to escape that feeling in a cycle that is not rational but is nevertheless true. Scare tactics may keep these boys clean for a while – a week, a couple of months maybe – but fear is only a temporary motivator. What these boys need is hope, inspiration, positive reasons not to use, and education about what affects porn use actually has on people in the long term.

Dear Allison and Deana,

I read about your project in the Times and I am a huge fan of what you are doing. I am a 24-year-old graduate now working in London, and it has been 2–3 years now since I have watched any porn. I am sending this email just in case I can help out with a few words on what giving up porn did for me ... I had watched porn since the age of 13 until the age of 22, and had concurrent issues with erectile dysfunction that I had always put down to being too drunk or being too nervous. It was only that I read about what porn can do to the brain on yourbrainonporn.com that I began to connect the dots. I even undertook 50 days of complete abstinence in order to 'rewire' myself ... I hope your talks are delivered with a heavy emphasis on how it is in the boys' interest to not watch porn, not just in the interests of the girls that they interact with. Abstaining from porn has brought me these benefits:

- I am much more attracted to women and attracted to more of them
- I have stronger connections with women
- I am much more confident around women
- Sexual performance has greatly improved
- Orgasms are ten times stronger

In the TEDx Talks and websites porn addicts have directed us towards, there is a lot of talk of neural pathways and neuroplasticity or brain plasticity. Gary Wilson, founder of pornonthebrain.com, defines neuroplasticity as: 'the lifelong ability of the brain to reorganise neural pathways based on new experiences. Neuroplasticity does not consist of a single type of brain change, but rather includes several various processes that occur throughout an individual's lifetime.' Wilson has an excellent TEDx Talk, in which he explains that the more men watch porn, the more their neural pathways become accustomed to the visual stimulation. These pathways become like well-worn highways, as they are travelled over and over again. This promotes an addiction to porn and leads to problematic sexual performance in real life intimate situations. Further, we ask if there is any scientific evidence that watching too much pornography causes actual harm to the brain to the person who is watching it? Yes. According to University of Cambridge neuropsychiatrist Dr Valerie Voon, the brain of a person addicted to porn exhibits the same changes as a person with a drug addiction.

So it appears that in the same way a drug addict 'craves' drugs, a person who becomes addicted to porn craves porn. In our brain, we have something called a reward centre. In our reward centre a chemical called dopamine is released, giving us a 'high' that we feel when we have accomplished something. Dopamine is released when one experiences moments of sexual excitement and novelty. Because porn contains so many 'novel' visuals, from the number of naked images that can be seen in a very short period of time, to the varying sexual acts portrayed, the more these images are reinforced, the more likely the user's sexual tastes will alter as well. Therefore this chemical that gives us such a 'high' gets triggered without having to do much to accomplish its goal. For years, scientists believed that at a certain point, our brains were 'fixed'; however, scans show that porn can actually alter the reward centre. This change in the reward centre triggers porn users to compulsively search for a new way to get this dopamine 'high'. As for someone taking drugs, who needs more drugs or a higher dose to produce the same high they first experienced, when someone watches too much pornography for them to experience a 'high', or sexual arousal, they need to have the boundaries pushed further to do so. They, too, develop a tolerance to it. This is a problem.

As parents, and as co-founders of The RAP Project, we believe that the taboo surrounding online porn needs to be lifted. There are different approaches to this, but open conversation about healthy relationships in contrast to porn seems to be unanimous. Dr Lisa Damour, an American psychologist specialising in adolescence, blogged some interesting advice: 'Pornography depicts one shadowy and loveless corner of the vast landscape of human sexuality. Your teenager might profess a sophisticated understanding of the many varieties of sexual activity, but there's still no harm in saying: "I know that a lot of kids are looking at porn online, but I'm hoping you won't. Sex can be mutual, loving and fulfilling and it can be dark, offensive and destructive. What you see in pornography is almost always the wrong kind of sex, and I don't want you getting the impression that that's what sex is all about."'

Here in the UK, more and more academics are calling for mandatory sex and relationship education (SRE). Dr Mark Limmer, a lecturer in public health at Lancaster University, wants SRE to reach beyond the biology and include positive, healthy messages about physical relationships. 'We do need children and young people to understand that sex has its place in a relationship, that it's pleasurable and intimate. Schools should take a healthy perspective on it.' If these topics are not taught, then he feels boys and girls may be drawn to pornography if their questions about sex are not met in the classroom.

What do we as mothers and as speakers to students recommend to parents? As unappealing as it may seem, most teenagers today have watched porn or do so regularly. Be bold, take five minutes to research porn online and get an idea of what they are consuming. And then speak to them in a non-judgemental way. If they are young, explain to them that they may come across a frightening sexual image by chance or a pop-up. Talk to them about it. If they are older, maybe hit home that this is not real, educational or what a healthy romantic relationship looks like. Remind your son that, according to *Men's Health* (March 2004), penis sizes are

30 per cent larger than average in porn, and 85 per cent of females have breast implants. Porn does not depict reality and it is purely visual. Also discuss the meaning of sexual consent. Teenagers know it is 16 here in the UK, but do they understand what it means?

Here's another story that resonates. A friend has two daughters: one 23 and another 16. She confided in us that she was very concerned about her younger daughter's romantic life. Something had changed over the past few years. Both girls were vivacious and attractive. Her eldest daughter, some five years earlier, dated in what our friend understood to be the 'normal' way, exploring romance and physical affection in much the same way as she herself had done in the early eighties. But her younger daughter, despite having a 'boyfriend', was not experiencing relationships in the same way. Strangely, her beau did not appear interested in intimacy beyond the odd stolen kiss. When the puzzled teenager asked close male friends what was going on, she was told that many young men were satisfied by watching porn. 'Most guys think it is easier that way, without the headaches of a real relationship.' As a result, the 16-year-old didn't feel good about herself, and suffered from insecurity and low self-esteem. The mother, understandably, felt concerned as she didn't want her beautiful daughter to be hurt or to feel in any way unattractive. 'What is going on? Why is it so different just five years on?' she asked us. Do young men really feel it is easier to watch porn than to engage in real life relationships? We suspect for some, the answer is yes. This is yet another reason why The RAP Project features a discussion on porn. Let's address it, not bury it.

PORN

Positive sexual intimacy is not reflected in porn

Own your bodies and your choices

Respect your partner's desires and boundaries

Neural pathways can be altered by watching too much porn

TOP TIPS

- Don't be embarrassed to talk about porn. Pitch the conversation so it is age appropriate and consider speaking to your children about porn from the age of 10
- Porn is not a sex manual. Would you learn to drive from watching the film *Fast and Furious 7*?
- Porn stars are not the average body type. Most breasts have been artificially enhanced and penises are some 30 per cent larger than the national average. Don't compare!
- Don't ever do anything you do not want to do. Own your body, own your choice

---

Resources

'The Great Porn Experiment', Gary Wilson (TEDxGlasgow)

http://yourbrainonporn.com/
garys-tedx-talk-great-porn-experiment

'Why I stopped watching porn', Ran Gavrieli (TEDxJaffa 2013)

http://tedxtalks.ted.com/video/
Why-I-Stopped-Watching-Porn-Ran

'Make Love Not Porn', Cindy Gallop (TEDxOxford)
http://tedxtalks.ted.com/video/
Make-Love-Not-Porn-Cindy-Gallop

Pornland: How Porn Has Hijacked Our Sexuality, Gail Dines (Beacon Press, 2011)

Your Brain on Porn: Internet Pornography and the Emerging Science of Addiction, Gary Wilson (Commonwealth Publishing, 2015)

6 Dating, Break Ups and Consent

'No means no, not convince me.'

Year 10 student

When the 15-year-old female student in our audience uttered this simple phrase, we were stunned. She spoke with passion and authority, revealing what many of our teenagers had tried to explain, using only six words. Young men, and in some cases young women, need to know when to stop their sexual advances. It's as simple as that. The RAP Project has evolved since its inception over two years ago, when our initial aim was to empower young people to own their sexual choices. And we still do. But now, when talking to teens about dating and sex, we realise that the concept of 'Just Say No' when you are asked or pressured into doing something that you are not that into is overly simplistic.

We listen to what teenagers have to say to us about what their lives are like growing up in the digital age and have adapted our presentations to reflect their concerns. Relationships, historically a tricky area for teenagers in any case, are now even more complex. 'Just Say No', advice passed down through generations, frankly doesn't carry the same weight as it once did.

The focus of our discussions with teenagers, in terms of sexual behaviour, tends to revolve around the concept of *consent*. The blurred lines and layered meaning of the word are more complicated than ever. It is common knowledge that legally the age of consent in England and Wales is 16, but what is crucial is that teens understand what that actually means. The US-based production company, Blue Seat Studios, produced a video comparing the concept of consent to offering someone a cup of tea. 'Consent. It's simple as tea', has received well over 2 million hits on YouTube (and counting) and combines efficiency and humour to illustrate the meaning of consent. Thames Valley Police have also promoted the video to highlight the issue of consent. If you offer to make a person a cup of tea and they affirmatively accept your offer, you make them a cup of tea. If they decline your offer, you don't. If they say yes but change their mind, you accept the fact that they don't want a cup of tea. If they wanted a cup of tea on Monday, it doesn't mean that they then want it on Tuesday. If they are sleeping or unconscious, you don't pour the cup of tea down their throat. Again, it is a simple concept, but it makes a lot of sense. Dozens of parents, students and especially teachers we work with speak excitedly about this as a highly effective video to share with their classes. We urge you to watch it as well: https://www.youtube.com/watch?v=pZwvrxVavnQ.

Sexual Assault

In our presentations, we feel strongly about the importance of clearly explaining the legal definitions of consent, rape and sexual assault. These words are used a lot, but the misconceptions of what they are and what they mean have been surprising and shocking. Also, we cannot forget the cultural differences among our audience. In one country, the meaning and age of consent will be different than in the UK. It is vital we define these.

> The elements of **rape** are:
> - A person (A) intentionally penetrates the vagina, anus or mouth of another person (B) with his penis;
> - (B) does not consent to the penetration; and
> - (A) does not reasonably believe that (B) consents.
>
> The elements of **assault by penetration** are:
> - A person (A) intentionally penetrates the vagina or anus of another person (B) with a part of their body or another object;
> - the penetration is sexual;
> - (B) does not consent to the penetration; and
> - (A) does not reasonably believe that (B) consents.
>
> The elements of the offence of **sexual assault** are:
> - A person (A) intentionally touches another person (B);
> - the touching is sexual;
> - (B) does not consent to the touching; and
> - (A) does not reasonably believe that (B) consents.

Interestingly, in terms of *consent*, there is no 'legal' definition, but the statute provides guidelines on ascertaining whether there was a lack of consent on the part of the victim. Consent means to give your permission freely, with 'freely' being the optimal word: to have something done to you or for you to do something to someone else sexually with no threats of any kind. And we are not just talking about physical threats, but manipulation, coercion or emotional blackmail of any kind as well. Lack of consent may be demonstrated by:

- The complainant's assertion of force or threats
- Evidence that by reason of drink, drugs, sleep, age or mental disability the complainant was unaware of what was occurring and/or incapable of giving valid consent
- Evidence that the complainant was deceived as to the identity of the person with whom (s)he had intercourse.

A boy or girl under the age of 16 cannot consent in law.

To illustrate what consent freely given means, we tell the story of Hannah, an outgoing 16-year-old girl. She had a crush on one of her best mate's older cousins. Jake was 25 and a bit of a bad boy. He asked her out on a date. She accepted. Flattered, she knew no one would approve because of Jake's age and reputation. As a result, she didn't even tell any of her friends, choosing to lie to everyone, making up a story that she was seeing some other boy that night. As you can guess, this is rarely a good idea.

We cannot stress enough how important it is to remind your teens that **someone reliable must know where they are and who they are with.** It is worth pointing out that this is not because we are being nosy and judgemental, but it is because we care for their well-being. Few teens can appreciate this, but we do need to have some idea of what they are up to in case things go wrong.

Hannah did not do this. She knew that her parents would not approve and that her friends, given Jake's reputation, would attempt to dissuade her from meeting up with him. Despite this, she agreed to meet him in the car park of a shopping centre. As they drove around, Jake realised that no one knew where she was and that they were alone together. He pulled the car off on to a dimly lit, deserted road. He opened his trousers and pulled out his penis. He instructed her on what he wanted her to do next. Shocked, she shook her head no. Jake then adopted a stronger tone, urging her to make him 'happy' and to 'get it over with'. If she did, he wouldn't tell anyone that she had sneaked out on a secret date with him. 'What would happen,' he threatened, 'if your parents found out? Well,' he leered, 'you probably wouldn't be allowed out of the house for a long, long time. And your friends, well, they're going to call you a slut.' He also threatened to send around a sexually explicit photo that she had texted to him earlier that week to everyone they knew. But, if she played by his rules, he would stay quiet. Hannah had thought that Jake really liked her and that he would be 'different' with her. She was terrified of what her family and friends would say or do if they saw the image of her. Petrified, she did what he wanted.

What we explain to young people is that in this situation Hannah's consent was not freely given. She was not physically threatened but she was blackmailed into performing a sexual act and therefore did not give consent. This is a crime. Many young people are surprised by this. Part of the problem of understanding the concept of consent is our misconception as a society about what rape and sexual assault actually look like. At one of our first talks at a school, we asked the question, 'What is rape?' A hand shot up straightaway and a student answered, 'Normal rape? You know, when a seedy-looking older man, wearing a trench coat, lurking down a dark alley, pulls a stranger to the ground and attacks her or him.' We understand this somewhat cinematic depiction of rape, but we explain that it is a fictionalised one. In fact, the majority of victims of rape and sexual assault know their attacker. According to Rape Crisis England & Wales, approximately 90 per cent of victims are familiar with their assailant.

Date rape

You also may have heard the term 'date rape'. A date rape is used to describe a situation when the victim and the assailant have a romantic link; it could even be a first date where there has not been a past sexual relationship between the people involved. By attaching any notion of 'romance' and dating rituals to this crime, it almost negates that what has happened was violent and controlling and makes it seems as if it is just 'sex that went wrong', and it is not. The misguided underlying theory of 'date rape' is that if two people are physically attracted to each other and are out alone together, there is some sort of implied consent that something sexual may occur. But we don't look at other crimes this way: if someone lives in a big house, it doesn't imply they are consenting to be the victim of a burglary; and if someone is walking on the street talking on their brand new iPhone, there is no implied consent that they want to be robbed.

Society's 'vision' of this crime correlates with why so many cases go unreported. In our presentation, we show a video produced by the Home Office of two teenagers going into a bedroom upstairs at a party to fool around. They are very familiar with each other, and exchange intimate hugging and kissing. It is clear they have a sexual, romantic relationship. But in the video, despite the young woman initially consenting to kissing and touching, she can clearly be heard saying, 'Stop it ... I don't want to' after the man pushes her down on to the bed and begins to undress her. He does not stop, and she is raped. The Home Office uses the young man's alter ego to shout at his criminal self from behind a glass window: 'Stop! She doesn't want to!' But the young man on the bed remains out of earshot, clearly breaking the law in what is quite a hard-hitting video for teenagers: https://www.youtube.com/watch?v=WIX9oREk8Fw.

The feedback we get from teens is insightful and, at times, disturbing. Many young people discount what they see on the video by saying that since the couple previously shared an intimate relationship, there is an assumption – an expectation – that something sexual would happen again. Therefore, some kids really do believe that if you have already consented to a sexual act in the past, future permission is carte blanche. Some other unfortunate comments we hear include that, as the young woman consented to initial kissing and caressing, anything that followed was consensual. Consent to a particular sexual act at a specific time should not be presumed to be continuous. So be clear with your kids: consent is finite and needs to be 'renewed' by the participants for different sexual acts at different times. Going back to the tea analogy, if you sit down to have a cup of tea with someone, and you offer them milk and sugar and they decline, you don't put it in their tea anyway. So if two people start kissing and one of them attempts to touch the other person's breast and she says 'No' or pushes the other person away, you don't do it anyway. Just because they want a cup of tea, it doesn't mean they also want milk and sugar.

There have been two extremely noteworthy TV documentaries surrounding these subjects broadcast in the UK since 2015: a Channel 4 documentary entitled 'Sex In Class' and a BBC Three documentary entitled 'Is This Rape? Sex On Trial'. In 'Sex in Class', Belgian sexologist Goedele Liekens is symbolically parachuted into a class of 15- to 16-year-olds in Accrington, Lancashire. Her goal is to openly discuss and assess their views on sex, porn, consent, sexual pleasure, etc. The lessons are extremely frank, visual and, at times, teachers as well as the students are clearly uncomfortable. However, Liekens argues strongly for more explicit sex education lessons in the UK. She also supports the introduction of an official GCSE on sex in the UK, as Britain has one of the highest rates of teenage pregnancies in the EU. During one lesson, Liekens discusses consent with the students and asks one young man whether if a girl consents to have sex with you, you are free to ejaculate in her face? He nods, 'Yes.' The girls in the room are somewhat pissed off with his response and a debate ensues. This is an extremely effective tactic, as their peers are saying to them directly 'this is not acceptable', rather than a middle-aged woman lecturing them on what is right and wrong. However, many of the teachers felt that she went too far. We also find a difference of opinion at schools. Some teachers are prepared to discuss porn and sensitive topics including anal sex, while others wouldn't dream of it. Our advice to those who ask is to listen to the teenagers. After our talks, both male and female teenagers approach the stage to ask us questions privately. All of them are acceptable, many of them highly sensitive and frank, a few absolutely shocking at the level of naivety, for example, 'You don't have to be 16 to consent to sodomy, right?'

The BBC Three programme 'Is This Rape? Sex On Trial' also garnered headlines after its broadcast. The documentary bravely attempted to question young people's attitudes to and knowledge of rape. The format placed 24 teenagers unknown to each other in two rooms separated by gender. They were then shown a video divided into three parts, followed by a courtroom drama. After each section, the male and female participants separately discussed and analysed what they believe happened. The teens had no access to social media or to the Internet. One of the dramatisations portrays two young people, Gemma and Tom, at a party. Gemma and Tom had previously been involved in a romantic sexual relationship and are seen separately at a house party. People are partying, dancing and flirting. Gemma is tipsy and tired, and falls asleep on the sofa. The re-enactment then depicts Tom crawling in under the covers next to her. She is clearly sleeping, but he wakes her by whispering in her ear and is seen laying very close to her. She rejects his advances by saying she wants to go back to sleep. He continues nevertheless and we are then to believe that he has put his penis into her mouth. She doesn't push him away or tell him to stop. She is clearly not, however, an enthusiastic participant. The events of the evening lead to Gemma calling the police to report that she has been raped by Tom. The participants in the BBC programme then vote as to whether they believe she had consented to oral sex.

Part Two of the video portrays Gemma, the alleged victim, and Tom, the alleged assailant, being questioned in court by a defence attorney. The leading questions are formulated in such a way to dispel a criminal act and to support consensual sexual activity. The final part of the dramatisation, portrays the lead questioning from the prosecuting attorney. The camera switches from Gemma's narrative of the event in question to Tom's different description of what happened on the sofa that evening. The prosecutor's line of questioning focuses on establishing that (and why) a crime was committed.

The participants in the documentary are then asked to vote on whether they believe a rape took place or if the act was consensual. Emotional and heated debate ensues, and the blurred lines prove complex. In the video, Gemma does not say 'No' to Tom's sexual advances, but nor does she agree to the sexual act. The issue is not as simple as to whether or not someone verbalises the word 'No' or physically pushes the other person away. It is also about understanding body language and whether someone is actually consenting and not just 'giving in' or 'giving up'. As we tell the young people we speak to, 'If you are confused as to whether someone wants to participate in a sexual act with you, wait for enthusiasm.'

In the end, 87 per cent of the participants voted that what they had witnessed was, under the law, rape. While the conclusion may seem straightforward, it doesn't adequately reflect the discussions that took place leading up to the 'verdict'. For example, many of the teens spent much time pondering the prior sexual relationship of Gemma and Tom. In some cases, mostly male, this former intimacy justified a view of presumed consent. The other issue that weighed heavily on the debate was the fact that Gemma did not clearly articulate the word 'No', cry out for help or push him away. One teenage girl called the incident a 'semi-rape'.

Unfortunately, and somewhat alarmingly, many of the participants agreed that the scenario was not that far-fetched.

Incidents similar to the one in the re-enactment depicted something similar that had either happened to them personally or to someone they knew. The RAP Project also comes across these cases. Many young women, and at times young men, describe situations where consent had not been given but, due to alcohol or assumption, sexual assault took place. Young men, rarely mind you, admit that perhaps they had made someone do something she or he did not want to do at one time or another.

What made this BBC documentary so potent in our opinion is that Tom and Gemma are just like the teenagers we speak to at every school we visit around the country. They are 'normal', sociable kids at a party, trying to build friendships or romantic relationships. What The RAP Project attempts to drive home to these kids is just how important it is to communicate clearly what it is you want. When you are old enough to have sex, you are old enough to discuss what you want to do. We tell the students over and over again that consent is finite, not a 'free pass'. If you are kissed passionately, it does not mean oral sex is a given. If you say yes to one sexual act it doesn't mean another is on the table, and if you say yes to sexual intercourse on Saturday night it does not mean the consent is still there on Monday morning. Our teenagers need to understand that each time, each act needs to be discussed and consent freely given. We always say, if you are mature enough to embark on a physical relationship, then you are mature enough to discuss what it is you want to do. Again, we promote the 'Friendship, Romance, Intimacy' approach as an alternative to building a healthy relationship on mutual trust.

The documentary brilliantly captures the confusion around 'consent' for teenagers today. We fear that the mixed messages inherent in online pornography and a lack of the legal understanding of the concept are big hurdles in our kids' sexual education. We hear these questions from our audience members at nearly every presentation, and we are proud to say that we are often thanked for clearly defining what the word actually means.

Communicating Consent

It is not new that teenagers, and even adults, in the romantic realm do not always clearly express their desires. After a presentation recently, a young man in Year 9 raised his hand to ask Allison the following: 'I get really confused by girls. What do I do? How do I know what they are saying? I have a friend who is a girl that I quite like. When she sees me, she tells me to "Go away!" The other day, at home after school, I checked my Facebook page. She had posted to me: "When I say go away, it means come closer." I mean, it is confusing.'

Pop culture expresses these dilemmas in several pop songs, most vividly in 'Blurred Lines' and 'What Do You Mean?' by Robin Thicke and Justin Bieber respectively. Have a listen, if you haven't already. As you have probably guessed, the crux of both songs is, 'I don't know whether you are saying no or yes, but actually I don't care because I know you want it'.

Educating young people on consent is crucial to their sexual development and this is an issue on both sides of the Atlantic. Some universities in the UK are now requiring that their students participate in 'consent' classes. In September 2014, the state of California enacted the 'Yes Means Yes' law to change the way colleges and universities investigate and prosecute sexual assault allegations. Instead of examining whether the victim articulated 'no' to his or her assailant, the law requires 'an affirmative, conscious and voluntary agreement to engage in sexual activity'. In December 2014, the National Union of Students (NUS) in the UK successfully launched the 'I Heart Consent' campaign, promoting a dialogue of affirmative consent between students. Some may feel that laws and campaigns encouraging and/or enforcing an affirmative verbal consent to sexual activity are a bit draconian, but if the underlying concern is whether consent is being given and how it is being communicated, setting up defined guidelines can be crucial to eliminate misunderstanding or even prevent a crime being committed. Though we fully agree with and support the consent-based programmes being launched at universities, we believe that the dialogue of consent must start at a much earlier age.

Is part of the reason for this 'miscommunication' the unhealthy images our teens get through the media? How often, be it in music videos, TV shows or in a movie, are we shown a 'struggle' between two very attractive young people? What appears to start out as a 'sexy' kissing scene turns to something less than romantic whereby the young woman begins to 'reject' the young man both verbally and physically. He, though, persists and she eventually 'gives in' to his 'powers of persuasion'. There are many examples of this: on the hit US series *Mad Men*, in the movies *The Back-up Plan* and *300: Rise of an Empire*, and most definitely in the smash hit series *Game of Thrones*. Women are portrayed as literally fighting off a man's sexual advances and eventually, after quite a violent struggle, 'giving in'.

Music videos and lyrics perpetuate – and even glorify – these images as well. In the song 'Animals' by Maroon 5, Adam Levine sings, 'Baby, I'm preying on you tonight / Hunt you down eat you alive.' In the highly sexual and violent video, the woman who the lead singer has been stalking is sleeping in bed. While she is in a deep sleep, he is seen stroking her body and kissing her. What is disturbing is then, later in the video, she is seen to be making passionate love to him. You are led to believe that these initial non-consensual acts lead to the man getting what he desires with the woman being a then willing participant. This is a further example of 'blurred lines' that are presented over and over again. Referring back to Thicke's 'Blurred Lines', he is singing to a woman telling her that he is better for her than her last guy because, 'He don't smack that ass and pull your hair like that.'

This leads us to a criminal case that Deana prosecuted back in New York where four young men were charged with rape. The defence was that, though the victim initially said no to their sexual demands, she then gave in to their 'powers of persuasion'. The case also illustrates other personal safety issues faced and choices made when dating. Zoe, 19 years old, meets 21-year-old Roger Cleaver during her first month at university. Having arranged a date, he collects Zoe from her home where he then meets her parents. In her rush to leave the house, nervous and excited, Zoe forgets to take her phone. Roger had originally arranged to take Zoe to the cinema and then for dinner, but he suggests a change of plan, and they meet up with his three male friends instead. Zoe agrees, as she desires to be popular and wants to be accepted. She interprets this as a sign that he really likes her. The five of them pile into Roger's car and while driving to an area of town she is not familiar with it dawns on Zoe that she doesn't actually know this man at all. Her gut instinct tells her that she should tell him to take her home, but she doesn't want to offend him and appear to be 'high maintenance' or rude. She ignores her inner voice.

Roger drives them back to his house to watch a movie and drink some beer. There had been a suggestion that other girls may join their party, but they never materialise. When they arrive, no one else is home. Roger leads them down to the refurbished basement. The men then try to convince Zoe to perform sexual acts on them. She refuses and is then raped by each of the four men. After it is over, Roger drives her home, much less the gentleman on the return trip.

When Zoe arrives at her front door, she goes immediately to her room and refuses to see anyone. Zoe experiences the feelings of many victims of sexual assault. After several days hiding away in her room, crying, feeling isolated, humiliated and blaming herself, Zoe eventually collapses into her mother's arms sobbing and the horrible details of that night come out.

This was one of the worst cases Deana ever worked on, for a number of reasons. Zoe, apart from being a lovely, polite and sensitive young woman, had, up until then, been a very enthusiastic fresher. She studied hard, earned money after school at a small shop and opted to go to a local university in order to live at home rather than accrue debt. She was thrilled to be asked out by this older, handsome student who was relatively popular around the campus. He appeared to be the all-American college boy with a supportive family and a great smile.

Zoe and Deana spent many hours going over what happened that night. In preparation for trial much of what they spoke of was about the choices Zoe made that night. What worried Deana was that the jury would judge Zoe more harshly than many of her other victims because of her choices. Choices that, in hindsight, people might say she shouldn't have made. But Zoe's choices were innocent. She had no idea that they would seriously impact the rest of her life. The fear was that Zoe would be torn apart by the defence attorney and Deana therefore went through an intensive line of questioning with her before she took the stand. Luckily, in Zoe's case the jury did not buy the defendants' claim that Zoe, though initially not consenting to the sexual acts being asked of her, eventually 'gave in' to the young men's powers of persuasion.

In terms of overall dating safety, Deana and Zoe spoke at length about many of the other choices she made that night. They discussed how well she really knew Roger, which of course she didn't. But, in reality, how well do we know anyone when we agree to go out on that first date? He seemed nice enough and there was no reason not to trust him. After all, they went to the same university. He looked like a nice guy. There is naivety in thinking that just because someone shares the same ethnic background, attends the same university and lives in a nice neighbourhood, they are trustworthy. Life would be easy if bad people fit a profile, but unfortunately they don't.

Zoe, a sensible young woman, went out without carrying her phone. We've all done that, right? Not a big deal? Wrong. Mobiles should always be on hand and fully charged in case your teen needs to reach out to someone or, on the other hand, be found. Yes, we know that they are using their phones for WhatsApp, texting and other social media, but they are essential in case of an emergency.

Zoe unfortunately ignored her gut instinct. She had only recently met Roger, didn't know his friends, didn't know where he lived and was outnumbered. She wanted to tell Roger to take her home, but she didn't dare as she did not want to upset or offend him in any way. Young people today want to be 'liked' more than ever before. Their self-worth equates to how many 'Likes' they get on Facebook or Instagram. They also strive to be popular, affable and easy-going. Although these are all lovely attributes, in terms of keeping themselves safe, those conciliatory qualities need to take a back seat to their well-being. Who really cares if they offend someone? We need to reinforce with our teens that being 'liked' should not define them and that if they feel uncomfortable in a situation, they need to remove themselves as quickly as possible. Make an excuse, such as, 'My grandma is sick', 'I need to go home to babysit my little sister' or 'My cat died'. Anything. Zoe wishes she had done that.

Zoe was also worried about what her parents would think of her if they knew the position she had found herself in. They always thought of her as sensible and she didn't want them to think otherwise. Our teens are under more pressure than ever before to be perfect, many of them striving for as many A*s as possible that they are desperately afraid of disappointing us. So they may not tell you when they are in a dangerous or vulnerable situation. We often say to teenagers that, if they find themselves in a difficult situation, they should call home because their parents 'ain't that bad'. We also remind them that although parents may not always like their choices, they will always love them. Getting into trouble with your mum and dad is a better option than getting into trouble with a stranger who could have a sinister motive in mind. Parents' memories are short in comparison with a teenager living with the memory of being the victim of a sexual assault.

Fortunately, many young people do choose the option of phoning a parent when weighing up their options in difficult situations. It is also a good idea to stress with your teen that a good, trusted and reliable friend (not necessarily their BFF) should know where they are and who they are with if they are not going to inform a parent, guardian or older sibling. Additionally, have a quick code word that they can text to that friend or parents if they find themselves in an uncomfortable situation. We say 'code' because of the following reasons:

- It should be a word that they can type very quickly
- If someone grabs their phone they won't know what the word means

They may never need to use this code, but it would be nice to know that if they do need to get out of a tricky situation, they have an exit strategy.

Dating and Personal Safety

Another issue that we are asked about is when should a young person trust someone enough to be alone with them? Teenagers today are faced with a number of dating dilemmas in terms of their personal safety. What constitutes a 'friend' as defined by Internet sites such as Facebook, and therefore how someone builds up trust, has radically changed the nature of relationships. Because our teens are of a generation where trust in relationships happens very quickly via social media sites, are they developing the skills needed to assess a person's integrity?

Kitty was 18 when she met someone who would change her life forever. She was working part-time at a local coffee shop. Every morning, a handsome young man would come in and order a double shot latte and make small chat with her. Patrick, Kitty thought, was 'adorable and personable'. Using her research skills, she found out he was 21 and worked at a local Internet software company. They flirted with each other for several weeks before finally arranging a date. She didn't think to mention this date to her mum or any of her friends. She didn't want to make a big deal out of it especially if the date didn't lead to anything further.

They met on a Thursday night at a bar she had always wanted to go to as it was one of the hottest new bars around. When she arrived, Patrick stood up and offered her a seat beside him. Kitty noted that Patrick appeared to be on a first name basis with the bar man and the waiters. 'He must be a regular here,' she thought.

Patrick was easy to talk to and they seemed to have a lot in common. Both enjoyed hiking, blues music and horror films. As the evening progressed, he told her what a great cook he was and suggested that, as his flat was only a couple of blocks away, he make them some of his infamous pasta puttanesca. The bar was getting louder and they were getting hungry, but Kitty wasn't sure what to do. She liked Patrick and didn't want him to think that she wasn't interested in him, but she really didn't know him very well. She thought, however, that since she saw him almost every day and he seemed like a nice guy, he must be a good guy. In addition, Kitty always thought of herself as quite a sensible girl who made good choices. She trusted her instincts. So far, Kitty had steered clear of trouble and thought that bad things didn't happen to people like her. She didn't want to seem prudish and unsophisticated, so they gathered their coats and bags and headed off to Patrick's flat. When they arrived, he opened a bottle of wine and started cooking. They had a lovely meal and great conversation. It was getting late and Kitty had an early start in the morning. She felt that the evening had gone very well and hoped that this was the start of something special.

As Kitty made her excuses to end the evening, Patrick told her that he was extremely disappointed that she wanted to leave. They started kissing and, as Kitty pulled away, Patrick got more aggressive. She pushed him away and he tugged at her clothes. He groped her in intimate places and tried to steer her back to the sofa. Luckily, Kitty was able to break free of his grip and, kicking madly and screaming, she managed to get out of his apartment before anything further happened. Understandably, Kitty was extremely shaken after the incident. A close friend who she called immediately afterwards convinced her to call the police. She did, and with her clothes being ripped and with visible bruising on her body, the police made a swift arrest.

This raises the important issue of at what point should teens allow themselves to let their guard down and be vulnerable with someone? There is no 'magic' moment or length of time. What we do say to teenagers, and frankly this can apply to anyone at any age, is that we would advise against finding themselves isolated with someone on the first couple of dates, even if they appear to be as gentle and trustworthy as Mahatma Gandhi. One example to give them, and in our experience seems to ring true with them, is the following: if someone new joins their class at school, they don't sit down next to them, plan to see them on their own that Friday night and then proceed to tell them the most intimate details of their life. That usually gets a bit of an ironic laugh from the kids. Teenagers seem to spend quite a long time building trust within their platonic relationships, so why then do they allow themselves to become vulnerable so quickly romantically? If anything, it should be the other way around.

Dating apps

This leads us to two popular dating apps that were first brought to our attention by a group of young women at a school we were working at: Tinder and Grindr. We had both heard of these apps and had adult friends who used them, but we had no idea that they were popular with teenagers until that day.

Tinder advertises itself as the app for 'how people meet. It's like real life, but better'. The way it works is that it allows you to view photos and profiles of people in your area. If you like their photo, you swipe to the left. If you don't, you can 'pass' them by swiping to the right. Swiping left gives you the opportunity to communicate with that person directly. Tinder has been nicknamed the 'hook-up' app.

Grindr is 'the world's largest gay social network'. To download Grindr the site says that you must be 18 years of age or over (occasionally 20 depending on the country the app is being accessed in). You must have an email account with Google to access the app. This is where your age can be verified. However, the same problem emerges. Anyone can fake their age and there are actually sites telling you how to do so. For example, the site www.deletegrindraccount.com goes into great detail with a step-by-step guide on how a young person under the age of 18 can access Grindr.

There are a number of safety concerns that arise when teenagers are using these apps. The first obvious one that springs to mind is the age of the other person they are meeting. A 15-year-old may think they are meeting up with another 15-year-old but, as there is no way to verify someone's age in advance, they are walking blindly into a potentially dangerous situation. Predators are very clever – they know how to create fake profiles and email addresses to lure young people in.

Also, if someone consumes alcohol they are more likely to take a risk and meet someone over one of these apps that they don't know. Alcohol makes many of us do things we would not otherwise do if we were not a bit 'buzzed'. At The RAP Project, we try to discourage young people from doing this. Again, we understand that to them meeting someone this way may seem 'normal' as they live their lives on social media. However, if they are going to meet someone via a dating website, they need to be of a sober mind and exercise sound judgement. If they are using Tinder and they want to swipe to the left, fine, just don't meet the person until you have time to think clearly about it and have done some investigating as to who this person may or may not be.

In any relationship, trust is vital. It is something that takes time. In terms of trusting when they feel comfortable to be alone with someone, your teen should be encouraged to take their time, establish trust and set up boundaries. If they are worth seeing again, the other person will not force them to make a decision that they are not comfortable with making yet. If the other person is putting pressure on them when they have only known them for a very short time, your teen needs to be strong enough to question the other person's motives. Teens need to be confident in their decisions and to be reminded over and over again to *own their choices*. Communication is key when dating. They need to be clear in their boundaries, so that there is no confusion.

Breaking Up Is Hard to Do...

As we know, most teenage relationships do not end up with them walking down the aisle together and we as parents and carers have always been there to mend the broken hearts. Usually when there is a break-up emotions run high regardless of who did the breaking up. We can relate to being on either side of the situation because, chances are, we have been on both sides in our life. When we had our hearts broken as a teen it was a fairly private affair; we had a bit of control over who found out about it and what they knew. The proof of your embarrassment, if you were embarrassed, could be destroyed and hopefully forgotten; love letters could be torn up and 'sexy' Polaroid photos destroyed. Yes, there was always gossip and whispers but now, with the use of social media, humiliation and heartbreak often goes viral. There seem to be additional, practical realities of break-ups in terms of social media that we did not have to deal with when we were growing up and we need to address these with our teens. Does our son or daughter really want to post the news of their breakup on WhatsApp, or to their 800 'friends' on facebook? When it comes to dating and social media teenagers need to understand the importance of discretion and privacy, and the fact that whatever they put out there stays there. Will and Lottie started dating when they were 16. They went to the same sixth-form college and had many mutual friends. They were sexually active and, on many occasions, Will in particular sent sexually explicit photos of himself to Lottie. Their relationship ended when they both left for university. Lottie was devastated over the break-up as it was Will's decision to terminate their relationship and she tried to contact Will a number of times. However, because he wanted a clean break from their relationship and wanted a fresh start at uni, Will was not attentive to her attempts to contact him. Lottie became angry and frustrated and, to get his attention, she started posting the explicit photos and messages he had sent her on social media sites. As could be predicted, it did not take long for these humiliating images to be found by students at Will's university. To say the least, this is not the way Will envisioned starting uni. He was humiliated by comments made by other students and by rude postings and messages. He stopped going to class and he ended up transferring to another university.

As of April 2015, legislation was enacted under the UK's Criminal Justice and Courts Act making the disclosure of 'private sexual photographs and films' of another person without their consent or 'with intent to cause distress' a criminal offence. The crime of 'revenge porn', as it is referred to, carries a sentence of up to two years imprisonment and/or a fine. We believe it is an important law and one that our teenagers need to be aware of. Hopefully it will help to deter behaviour like Lottie's as, in situations like this, the damage to the victim's reputation and emotional well-being can be devastating.

We also want to remind our teenagers that break-ups happen to everyone. It may feel like the end of the world, especially in cases of first love, but like all of us, they will survive. Some take break-ups better than others. Don't let your teen be too hard on themselves and remind them to love themselves, keep busy, see friends, go to the cinema and take hot baths if they are down. As parents we can also play a role in their emotional recovery by taking them to lunch, shopping or for a walk with the dog.

DATING

Do your homework. Know who you are going out with, their phone number, address and where they go to school

Alcohol impairs and affects your ability to assess risk

Tell a reliable friend who you are going out with and where you are going

Isolated? Don't be. Keep first dates in public places

'No' means 'no', not 'convince me'

Gut instinct: follow it – we cannot stress this enough

TOP TIPS

- Avoid hook-ups. Remember, friendship, romance then intimacy works best
- Have someone check in to give you an 'out' if you want to end the date
- Remember: Mutual respect, mutual consent
- Avoid parks during the evenings as they can be dangerous
- Be discreet: don't post details about your date or your bust up
- Self-care is key when your relationship ends

Resources

Disrespect NoBody

www.disrespectnobody.co.uk/

Family Planning Association

www.fpa.org.uk

Loveisrespect

www.loveisrespect.org

NHS: Abuse in Teenage Relationships

www.nhs.uk/livewell/teengirls/Pages/relationshipviolence.aspx

TeensHealth

www.kidshealth.org/en/teens/family-abuse

7 Parties, Pitfalls and Music Madness

'I had years of partying, and I was kind of surprised and happy I survived it all. Now, being a parent, I look back on it thinking, "Oh God. The things you did!"'

Jeff Bridges

B y now, you will hopefully have a clearer idea of how to speak to your teenagers in the digital age. We've looked at the shift in sexual and romantic relationships, and have examined how the easy access to hard-core pornography is influencing expectations. We have also considered how social media places our teenagers under tremendous pressure. In this chapter, we are moving into more familiar territory – parties – and, like our generation, Bacchus beckons at roughly the same age. We find the teenagers we speak to begin going to house parties in Years 9 and 10 (aged 14 or 15). These gatherings vary greatly, as they did in our day. Different parents have different rules. When we first began visiting schools, a few heads and deputy heads asked us to address parents on drinking laws and to stress the importance of parental supervision at parties. They found that a number of students often came in rather 'wrecked' on a Monday morning if they had been at a particularly wild party that weekend. But having discussed it among ourselves, we realised this was going to be tricky to negotiate: The RAP Project ventures into difficult territory during each presentation, but we are not in the business of telling adults how to run their domestic lives.

Subsequent conversations unveiled another layer to an already complicated relationship between parents and schools. Who is responsible for educating our teenagers about the dangers of underage sex, consent and alcohol consumption? Should parents allow sleepovers of both sexes? Do parents have the right to provide alcohol to underage teens if they wish? If so, do they have an obligation to inform the parents of the kids who are invited? Should under-18s bring alcohol to a party? We even differ slightly on our own approaches to some of these questions, and there is no doubt that every family has its own set of rules.

One 13-year-old described a party she attended with parents present. On offer were soft drinks, crisps and punch. The punch proved quite popular and some took to guzzling as much as possible. Apparently, one of the parents had added some red wine to the punch. The parents hosting the party did not inform the parents of those invited that alcohol was being served. Once this became public, several mothers and fathers were out-raged. 'Why on earth would 13-year-olds knowingly be offered alcohol?' and 'Why weren't parents asked first?' were two of the common reactions. We, like the schools we work in, do not promote or condone underage drinking. However, we know that it happens and feel that it needs to be addressed with eyes wide open.

When speaking to parents or to their teenagers, we at The RAP Project share real life scenarios that teens have been privy to. We discuss statistics about alcohol and sexual assault, the powerful drug Rohypnol and the realities of how parties can get far more out of control without adults on the scene. We also clarify what the UK's laws are on underage drinking, as well as underlining that the UK's Chief Medical Officers recommend an alcohol-free childhood as the healthiest and best option. But, of course, it is then up to individuals to make their own decisions. (Drinkaware, an independent charity aiming to reduce alcohol-related harm by helping people make better choices about their drinking, explains the law on its website: www.drinkaware.co.uk.)

When we speak to our audience, we have to be realistic. Many young people are going to drink before they are 18. We have lived in the UK for many years and it is no surprise to anyone that Britain can be a boozy country. To give you a better idea, the Offending, Crime and Justice Survey undertaken in 2015 shows that 56 per cent of the 5.4 million youngsters aged 10 to 17 in England and Wales admitted drinking in the past year, including 3 out of 10 children in the 10 to 13 age group. A total of 48 per cent said they had got the drink from their parents, while 23 per cent of those getting 'very drunk' at least once a month said their main source of alcohol was their parents. Allison has also witnessed some resourceful 15-year-olds asking a homeless person camped outside of the local Tesco to buy vodka on their behalf, 'tipping' him with a can of Guinness and a sandwich. Where there is a will, there is a way.

On the other hand, many teenagers, for religious or simple taste reasons, will not touch the stuff. And others do not want to lose control. This is the healthier, safer option for young people. One 16-year-old daughter of a friend is a keen football league player who loves to socialise with her friends. Despite her conscientious approach to her GCSE preparation and heavy footie training schedule, she still finds time to go to at least one party a week. She does not touch alcohol yet sticks around as some of her friends partake. 'It's a laugh, watching them gradually get more and more out of control,' she says. 'Aren't you ever tempted?' we ask her. 'Not one bit,' she says.

House Parties

When Allison's son has house parties, three in the space of two years, they usually consist of 20 or so 17–18-year-olds. Pizza, music, dancing, wine and vodka are available, though the adults refrain from providing any alcohol. Allison and her husband stick around, watching a movie upstairs in order to give the teenagers some space. By midnight at one of these parties, Allison felt it was time to wrap up the festivities. The partygoers were in good cheer and enjoying themselves, but one young man had been sick in the loo and two of his mates were looking after him, one wiping his brow with a wet cloth. Allison decided to send everyone home but did allow a few people to sleep on the sofas and the floor. Unfortunately for the hosting parents, a small percentage of teenagers are inevitably going to experiment, push the envelope and, as a result, make a bit of a mess.

Deana hosted a house party for her then 14-year-old daughter. Her husband was there, as well as three additional adults to help chaperone. There was, to their knowledge, no alcohol present at the party. None of the adults left the house throughout the evening and Deana has often referred to it as being like 'patrol duty' with the NYPD. Despite their best efforts, however, alcohol was consumed. How did this happen? There are a couple of theories. The first, bottles were smuggled in via the guests' rucksacks. Deana would have never considered searching invitees' bags at the front door, as she had heard other less trusting parents have done. The second possibility is that friends stopped by earlier in the day under a false pretence: 'Can we help set up?' or 'I just wanted to say "Hi"' when in fact they were stashing the booze in the garden or behind a bin. Clever, eh? If only they spent as much time figuring out maths equations! Luckily no vomiting or other serious incidents occurred that night. Parents came to collect their kids, who were all fortunately in one piece, at the end of the evening.

Eventually, we are going to have to trust our teenagers and leave them on their own with friends. How else will they learn to become responsible adults? It is a risk, sometimes at a cost, but parties are a part of growing up – a fun, healthy way for our kids to personally interact, socialise and create memories. With the number of hours many teenagers spend on social media, these parties are essential building blocks for real life friendships. Remind your teens that the legal drinking age is 18 and, if and when they do imbibe, to please eat. Worrying about fitting into those skinny jeans is no excuse to skip a meal. Food is essential. Also, tell your children to remember to drink plenty of water or soft drinks in between anything alcoholic. Like it or not, shots are popular, and a sure-fire way to get sick.

Two 17-year-old teenage boys confirmed this theory. They took turns rather gleefully explaining to us how shot glasses, a deck of cards and bottles of booze were key ingredients to a successful house party or even a party in the park. One popular drinking game called 'Ring of Fire' dictates a player downs a shot in one according to the card drawn. If a player pulls a 'four', this means 'whore', dictating the female players in the circle must drink. 'Six' means 'dicks', which means the males have to drink. It gets worse, I'm afraid. During the game, everyone is invited to add a splash of chosen tipple, be it vodka, rum, Scotch, etc. to a single glass. This is called a 'dirty' shot. Another drinking game is 'Ride the Bus'. The dealer asks players 'red' or 'black', then the colour of the card dictates who drinks or not. No wonder people are getting sick. Or out of it. Or worse…

We asked some of our interns to undertake research by questioning their 15–17-year-old peers on the subject of drinking and drunk behaviour. Some responses were more surprising than others:

- 'Boys always want to get girls drunk so that they can take advantage of them.'
- 'Almost all my sexual experiences have occurred as a result of alcohol.'
- 'Boys keep asking if you want more to drink, insisting until you are past any point of sobriety. They seem to think they will then have an easier chance to fool around and, sadly, they are right.'

- 'Girls sometimes like to get boys drunk. It is not just guys who do this type of thing. We always get blamed for this kind of behaviour but, believe me, girls can get up to the same kind of stuff.'

Some of the responses were disturbing:

- 'A friend had passed out and a guy she had once dated was all over her, or rather all under her clothes, touching her up.'
- 'I was very drunk. A boy came into the bathroom and kissed me. I didn't want to but I could not get him off me. He even put his hands down my pants. I tried to get out of the bathroom but he stopped me. Finally someone started knocking and he stopped.'
- 'I know many people who have sex while being drunk – it's very common for two people to sleep together these days who aren't together as a couple.'

Alcohol and sexual assault

When The RAP Project was in its infancy, we invited teens and parents to hear what we had to say at focus groups. One mother asked us to remind our kids that alcohol can act as a date rape drug. Shortly afterwards, an experienced deputy head concurred: 'Young men and women experimenting with alcohol aren't always aware how personalities can radically transform when drinking. You might be a timid, kind person one minute and then sexually aggressive the next.'

According to studies undertaken by the Royal Colleges of Physicians and the Home Office, alcohol is a major factor in sexual assaults. It is no surprise that, according to a report issued by the Office for National Statistics entitled 'Focus on: Violent Crime and Sexual Offences, 2011/12', 32 per cent of women who had been sexually assaulted had been under the influence of alcohol. The same report stated that the victims reported that 47 per cent of the perpetrators were also under the influence of alcohol. According to a study undertaken by the Royal College of Physicians. Use of alcohol by both victim and perpetrator is commonly implicated in sexual assault, although the state of intoxication of the victim is more significant. The proportion of reported rapes in which alcohol use is reported or can be detected biochemically in the alleged victim varies from 35 to 46 per cent. In one study, the measured blood alcohol level for 60 per cent of cases raised questions as to whether the victim would be in a position to give informed consent. Where alcohol has been used by a perpetrator of sexual assault, there is likely to be a greater degree of sexual abuse and it is more likely to be associated with physical injury.

Intake of alcohol by an individual increases the risk of both stranger rape and date rape occurring. Factors contributing to this may include the misinterpretation of friendly cues as sexual invitations and diminished coping responses in the victim, leading to an inability to ward off unwelcome advances. Alcohol consumption alters risk perceptions as well as lowering inhibitions. At the same time, perpetrators may actually seek out intoxicated women.

With this in mind, we ask all of our teenagers who might choose to drink to please practise self-awareness. Yes, they may pretend to listen to what we have to say and let it go in one ear and out the other, but if they can remember this advice, it will help them. We ask them to monitor how their bodies metabolise alcohol. Do they get tipsy quickly? Do they get sick? Do they change, become aggressive or hostile? Black out? If they understand and can monitor how their body processes alcohol, they can counteract these potentially dangerous side effects by drinking more water, less booze and knowing when to call it a night. To wake up somewhere and not know what happened is not safe and, with social media playing such a massive role in our kids' lives, there can be additional tragic outcomes.

Drinking alcohol does not in itself lead to a sexual assault but getting drunk affects our ability to make sensible, safe decisions. When we get drunk, we decrease our ability to fight off an attack – any attack, not just sexual. And while this may seem all too obvious to our teenagers, the ability to clearly communicate is jeopardised. Teenagers need to fully understand consent. When at a party, when maybe a couple go for a walk to get some fresh air or want to kiss in a bedroom, things can get steamy. Both parties need to say 'Yes' or 'No' to a sexual act. Slurring is not the language of consent.

What follows is a shocking, horrible and unfortunately true story about a 15-year-old girl. All names and some other details have been changed to protect the privacy of those involved. The party scene was just kicking off for these teens, and Jane was thrilled to be invited to Simon's party, a friend she had known since primary school. Jane and her best friend Vicky had carefully calculated a plan. Jane told her parents she was staying at Vicky's, and in turn Vicky told her parents she had been invited to stay at Jane's. Up to this point, they had been honest with their parents and both parties believed their daughters and did not check out their stories. The night began with a great sense of excitement and anticipation. The selected 'invitees' knew Simon's parents were out of town, so anyone who wanted to could sleep over. And as these teenagers, the majority 15 years of age, were only just starting to experiment with alcohol, there was a sense of the unknown, an element of danger. Jane and Vicky felt no guilt about lying to their mums and dads about where they were. 'What could possibly go wrong?' they thought. Simon's parents were pretty lenient and allowed him to have friends over from time to time even if they were out of town. He did have an older brother, 18-year-old Jack, but he preferred hanging out at the pub. Jane and Vicky normally had to wake up early to attend athletic competitions on the weekends, but this weekend was going to be different. These girls wanted to see what the cool kids at school were talking about on Monday mornings.

When the girls arrived at the party, Jane felt a frisson when Simon and Billy opened the door. Both young men, slightly older at 16, were quite fit and very popular. Jane had always had a bit of a crush on Simon. He approached her with open arms and gave her a bear hug, then offered her a beer. Taking a big gulp, she hoped it might take the nervous edge off. This was new territory for her. From the corner of her eye, Jane saw Vicky and some others talking animatedly.

The party soon transitioned into a rave, as more and more people filed in through the front door. Jane sensed a loss of control and panicked. Simon spotted her, walked over and reassured her that everything was okay. 'Some idiot posted the party on Facebook. Would you like to play a drinking game with some of us in a less hectic space?' he asked. Jane, having lost track of Vicky, nodded and was led into a bedroom. She had never tried vodka and had not eaten since breakfast. Five partiers huddled together in a close circle and played 'Truth or Dare', followed by shots. Suddenly Jane felt very drunk. Feeling ill, she could barely stand up. She found the loo, threw up violently, crawled into a bedroom and passed out. When she awoke the next morning at 6am, she had no recollection of the night before. She had a horrific headache. Why were her clothes off? Her bra and T-shirt were next to her on the bed, while her jeans and knickers had been pulled down to her ankles. What she couldn't understand at all were the odd black markings smudged all over her body. Jane tried to read what she guessed were letters, but everything was a blur. She felt sick.

Wobbly on her feet, she gathered her belongings and climbed her way out of Simon's house. Downstairs was trashed. The combined odour of stale alcohol and cigarettes sickened her. She gingerly walked over sleeping bodies and let herself out. Dazed, she walked home and went straight into her bedroom to undress and then shower. In the mirror, she could not understand why there were black smudges over her breasts, stomach and backside. 'What the hell happened?' she wondered. After scrubbing herself, she climbed into bed. As soon as she fell asleep, her mobile phone rang. Vicky sounded emotional, saying there were pictures of Jane naked with rude words scribbled all over her body on Facebook and Instagram. Jane was horrified, humiliated and extremely embarrassed. She had no memory whatsoever of the night before. 'Why would anyone do this to me?' she wondered. Hadn't she been with trusted friends she had known since primary school? She refused to go to school that Monday, turned her phone off and would not leave her room. Jane's mother was concerned but put her daughter's dramatic behaviour down to an argument with a friend over a boy or something. Jane had not told her what had happened.

At school, however, a teacher sensed heightened activity with phones and confiscated one during class. She saw the photos of Jane and reported it to the head. No one would admit to taking the pictures or name the person who wrote the abusive messages all over Jane's body. The slurs included 'slut', 'pig' and 'slag'. Circulating nude or explicit images of someone under the age of 18 to others is against the law. Suddenly, this 15-year-old girl who lied to her parents about where she was spending the night and who had so looked forward to a party at a boy's house was the centre of an embarrassing, humiliating and very serious investigation.

Jane had done what so many teenagers do: she had been excited to go to a party with no parents present where she could experiment with alcohol and maybe a cigarette. Perhaps she would have her first kiss that night, she hoped, or maybe get asked out on a date. Her mother and father were horrified at the level of shame their daughter, now in hospital, had to deal with. They supported her throughout her ordeal and the obscene pictures were finally taken down from the Internet. The technical teams at Facebook and Instagram helped remove them from their sites and any student caught sending them was threatened with expulsion.

Smartphones with cameras are now as much part of the social scene at parties as music. While Jane's story is an extreme one, there are plenty of photos and videos illustrating inappropriate or embarrassing incidents. Fortunately for our generation, we did not have our own behaviour documented in this way. It is so important to remind your kids to be careful not to be caught on camera doing anything that will embarrass them or hurt them at a future time.

THE DOORMAN

Another fixture becoming increasingly more common at teenage parties is the 'doorman'. With social networking, parties are rarely 'by invitation only'. Party invitations get shared online and can go viral via WhatsApp or Facebook. Suddenly, a friend of a friend of a friend arrives, and the numbers can grow out of control. Some clued-up parents are asking friends or older sons, or even hiring a young man, to stand at the door of a party to check names against the guest list. Allison's son worked the door recently and he earned his £30. He said the gig was much more difficult than he imagined. Realising the evening was not going to be straightforward, he enlisted a close friend to come and help. Both young men had to turn away at least 30 people not on the list and unfortunately some turned quite aggressive. One kid intimated that he had a knife and insisted he would get inside. The doormen talked him down, but it took some negotiating. The parents were inside, but if your teen is planning a large party after GCSEs or A level exams, hiring a friend of the family to check names off a list may not be a bad idea.

Drugs

Part of our RAP presentation has to address legal and illegal highs. It is no secret that if parents are not present at parties, drug dealers are more likely to show up, and dealers are not around to make teenagers feel good, but rather to make as much profit as possible. Rat poisoning, talcum powder, laxatives and anaesthetics are just a few of the ingredients used to lace drugs and increase the weight of the product. Many drug dealers actually name their drugs or put a symbol on the package, like a skull and crossbones. Looking back at the tragic death of award-winning actor Philip Seymour Hoffman, the press widely reported the large quantity of heroin in his apartment. The plastic packets were emblazoned with an ace of spades or ace of hearts. Young people having a good time on a night out are dealers' prime targets and anything can go wrong, from a serious allergic reaction, leading to long-term physical or mental illness, to a senseless death. In February 2014, 17-year-old Regane MacColl fell ill at a nightclub in Glasgow. She was taken by ambulance to the city's Royal Infirmary for emergency treatment but died shortly afterwards. Her death is being linked to red pills known as Mortal Kombat or Red Dragons. These pills have a dragon embossed on one side and are believed to contain deadly levels of a super-strength amphetamine. These tablets have been linked to a number of fatalities.

If parents are around at a house party, then drug dealing and consumption are less likely to happen. But again, if people want to take drugs, they will find a way. A well-known photographer lost his son a few years ago in north London. The 17-year-old boy, Joseph Benett, was happy, healthy and on track with his A levels. He went to a party and inhaled what he thought was laughing gas. Laughing gas, or 'hippy crack', is nitrous oxide, a legal high that gives users a brief feeling of intense euphoria. It is very popular with mothers in labour, dental patients and with youngsters at parties, festivals and clubs. The Home Office reports that nearly half a million young people aged between 16 and 24 have used it in the last year. Tragically, Joseph inhaled a chemical cocktail that included butane and suffered a heart attack. Allison has found used laughing gas canisters in her garden and has spoken to her kids about its dangers.

Research online says nitrous oxide is dangerous when mixed with alcohol and FRANK, a well-respected information and advice service which spells out the dangers and effects of drugs to young people and parents in a brilliant manner, warns there is a risk of death as a lack of oxygen can occur when using nitrous oxide. This risk is likely to be greater if the gas is consumed in an enclosed space or if a substantial amount is rapidly inhaled.

As of midnight on 26 May 2016, the production, distribution, selling or supplying of New Psychoactive Substances (NPS), or what are commonly known as 'legal highs', is now illegal. Conviction under the Psychoactive Substances Act carries a jail term of up to seven years in prison. What are NPS? They are a synthetically manufactured substance designed to replicate the same effects as illegal drugs such as heroin or cocaine. Taking one of these substances can lead to psychotic episodes.

'LEGAL' HIGHS

- Spice/Black Mamba: replicating the doping effect of cannabis, these are two of the brands known to cause paranoia, delirious ranting and hallucinations
- Laughing gas: otherwise known as nitrous oxide, laughing gas comes in canisters and is used recreationally after being inhaled, often out of balloons. It gives users a light-headed, euphoric feeling that lasts for several seconds, but, due to it depriving the body of oxygen, can be fatal when taken in excess
- Salvia: unlike other synthetic legal highs, salvia comes from a plant. It is still sold in many so-called 'headshops'. When chewed or when dried and smoked, it can create a hallucinogenic experience

Rohypnol

The other drug we are obliged to discuss, especially with the older students hitting the legal age of 18, is Rohypnol, commonly called 'roofies' or the date rape drug. Rohypnol is a very powerful sedative, prescribed as a sleeping pill, and has anaesthetic qualities. The drug is odourless, tasteless and dissolves easily in carbonated drinks, wine, cocktails, and even water. The British medical community prescribes it as Flunitrazepam. It is illegal in the USA, but considered a class C drug here in the UK and only legal when prescribed by a GP. The effects can last for up to 4–12 hours and cause partial amnesia. According to the NHS, other commonly used drugs are ketamine, an illegal horse tranquilliser, and GHB (gamma hydroxybutrate), an illegal human tranquilliser.

Sex offenders take advantage of these drugs as victims cannot normally recall the assault or events surrounding the incident. Because of this amnesiac effect, there are no official government statistics on how often these date rape drugs are administered. As the drugs only stay in the person's system for a short period of time, the chance of detecting their existence is slim. However, both Deana and Allison know people, the majority female, who have been given Rohypnol in their cocktails. When we ask students if they have ever heard of this drug, the majority of the Years 12 and above put their hands up. When we ask if anyone in the room knows of anyone who has been given Rohypnol, we often hear from a teacher or a student who knows a young man on a gap year abroad, a friend, a mother or maybe an older sister who has been 'roofied'.

Men and women we know who have had their drinks spiked describe the sensation as follows: they suddenly feel as if they have downed two bottles of wine with pills, they cannot speak or stand without the help of someone and are physically and mentally incapacitated. Instinct tells them to get some air or go to the toilet to try to vomit and rid their body of the drug. This, of course, is very dangerous, as anyone who manages to get outside can easily be led into a car. Anyone in a loo at a noisy club can be followed and locked into a cubicle. We preface the Rohypnol section in our RAP presentation by saying this drug is not everywhere and you are not necessarily ever going to come across it. But it is important to know it *is* out there, especially in clubs, pubs and particularly at university parties. Two victims we know were older, their drinks spiked at work parties.

This a story shared with us by a 21-year-old woman who, at the outset, had felt fortunate to get a work experience placement at a large advertising agency post university. We will call her Jenny. Having just graduated, she was not yet sure of her career path and was thrilled to have landed this plum gig. Naturally gregarious, she became quite friendly with a couple of other people in her section of the office. The company employed young, hip people from all over the world. She was invited to her first office party, given to celebrate the closing deal of a winning campaign. The party was held at a trendy restaurant near the office. Jenny had arranged to stay with a colleague, Nina, as Jenny's flat was on the other side of town. Nina had been working at the firm since graduating with flying colours from university a couple of years earlier and lived nearby. Jenny, a bright and ambitious young woman, was determined to show her boss that she was mature and could be taken seriously. Jenny was keen on not drinking too much and on making a good impression all around. At the party, she had one glass of white wine and mingled with her new colleagues and various executives. Later, during a conversation with an older man from the head office, she felt her body go limp and she became very disorientated. She vaguely remembers him ushering her out of the party and into a taxi. The executive followed her into the cab and the taxi drove off.

The next morning Jenny woke up in a hotel room, alone, naked, bruised and disorientated. She knew she had been raped. Gathering her clothes, she left the hotel and flagged down a taxi to get home. She scrambled through her front door, bathed and threw the clothes from the night before into the rubbish bin. Jenny felt deep shame and humiliation. On the following Monday, Jenny phoned the receptionist at the advertising company and made an excuse that for 'personal reasons' she would not be returning to complete her work experience. She did not tell her mum, with whom she was very close, nor report it to the police or seek medical help. Having had one glass of wine and then Diet Coke all night, she knew she had been 'roofied'. She had never before blacked out nor had any recollection of what happened. She chose not to report the incident as she felt ashamed and guilty in some way. Jenny did nothing wrong. The perpetrator committed a crime. She chose not to go to the hospital or the police. This is not rare.

One very important word of advice we tell our children and the kids in our sessions is: do not leave your friends behind, even if they say they are having the time of their life and will be fine. Compromise, negotiate a leaving time and stick together. Criminals who want to dose someone with this drug know what they are doing. Someone left on their own is much more likely to be a target. The evidence is clear. The number of people 'roofied' with a friend at their side who have then made it home safely is higher compared to those who choose to stay on at a club or pub on their own. But this is not black and white. As we saw from Jenny's story, it can happen at a work do, at a freshers' party or at a club whether one is on their own or not. Please tell your teens to keep their drinks, be it Diet Coke, white wine, beer or whatever, with them at all times. Take it to the loo, carry it on the dance floor and, when holding it, always use your hand to cover the top of the glass.

One story that we'll discuss in more detail in Chapter Nine shocked the hell out of us: an incident occurred at the University of Oxford where Pembroke College rugby club's social secretary sent an email inviting players to 'pick' a female fresher for a night out and spike her drink with a date rape drug. Then, much to our surprise, Bloomingdale's, New York's well-loved and established high-end store, also chose to make light of a date rape drug in a very poorly executed holiday ad campaign that suggested spiking a friend's eggnog. This ad was quickly withdrawn.

Likewise with rape jokes, when did spiking someone's drink, which is against the law, become a trendy, sporty, funny, media-friendly subject? To be more precise, under Section 61 of the Sexual Offences Act 2003 it is a specific offence for a person to administer a substance to somebody (or to cause somebody to take a substance) without their consent and with the intention of stupefying or overpowering them, in order to enable the offender or any other person to engage in sexual activity with them. This offence carries a maximum sentence of 10 years' imprisonment. It is worth noting that the definition of a 'substance' can also include alcohol. It's just not funny. Ask Jenny.

Look Out for Each Other

Back to Jane and Vicky, the guests at Simon's party. These girls did not have an exit plan that night, which is something we strongly advise to all of our students. In an age when plans are often made last minute via social media, friends need to map out their night and understand how they are travelling to and from a house party, club or bar. Why not agree first on a time to leave together? Obviously plans may change, but stick together.

We promote the notion that 'Chivalry is Sexy'. Not the old-fashioned chivalry where the knight in shining armour looks after his damsel in distress, but modern men and women taking care of each other and making sure they are okay. In the personal safety section of our Social Skills presentation, we make a point in suggesting that if a friend has been missing for over 25–30 minutes, why not go and look for him or her? Maybe Sophie is passed out in a bedroom or John is sick as a dog in the garden. 'If one of you were in a vulnerable situation', we ask, 'wouldn't you want a friend to help or make sure you were safe?' The students nod in agreement. In Jane's situation, the girls did not look out for one another. Young and inexperienced, they had no idea this could ever happen to one of them, let alone to anyone, anywhere. Again, what happened is not Jane's fault or Vicky's for not thinking about where Jane might be. But why not tell your teens to look out for one another?

Using her background as a former sex crimes prosecutor, Deana devised a non-judgemental storytelling technique to illustrate how people's decisions can maximise or minimise risky choices. We call one case story 'It Can't Happen to Me' … Imagine four 16-year-old girls seeking adventure. They set themselves a challenge: could they get served in a pub? Taking time to dress and do their make-up immaculately, they leave for the pub, with a plan to go home together. To their surprise, the barman pours them drinks. Three of the girls want to hear the band playing at one end of the pub. One of the girls, Debbie, stays at the bar. She is standing at the bar, sipping on her glass of Pinot Grigio and enjoying finally feeling 'adult'. Then she buys another drink. A handsome man strikes up a conversation with her and they chat amiably. Time flies and the closing bell signals that it is time to go home. Debbie leaves the bar area and looks for her friends. She rings them, but all their phones go directly to answerphone. Returning to the bar, her new friend senses that something is not right. 'Is everything okay?' he asks. 'Not exactly,' she replies. 'My friends have left without me'. 'Oh, well, I can give you a lift. Is it far?' Looking back, Debbie will remember this moment very clearly. At the time, she considers her options. She could call home, explain to her mother that she has been drinking all evening at a pub and her friends have abandoned her. This option would leave her grounded, the target of much parental discipline and, in short, is not terribly appealing. But if she chooses to get a lift with this man, she would be taking a risk. 'But bad things don't happen to smart girls like me. I am doing Further Maths after all,' Debbie says to herself, and she accepts the man's offer of a lift. The man stops off at his place along the way and asks if she needs the loo. She says yes and, once inside, he sexually assaults her. It is a decision that will remain with Debbie for the rest of her life.

One of the personal safety lines we repeat throughout our presentation is to 'Stick to the Plan'. If you are leaving with a set of friends, don't deviate at the last minute unless there is a very good reason. Teens should always keep some extra money for a taxi or to top up their travel card. As we mentioned in Chapter Two, we call this 'emergency funds'. Emergency funds do not mean 'I am hungry and want a kebab', but rather a little cash stashed away, behind their travel card or in their wallet so that they can get home safely at the end of the night. Just as we remind our own kids to call us if they get into a jam when out on the town, we tell the teens in our talks to call their own parents if they are in trouble. 'We may not always like your choices, but we love you and want you to be safe.' Getting into trouble at home for a week or two is a lot less catastrophic than having to live with a very difficult memory for the rest of their life.

The excitement of going to parties for our teens for the first time, in Years 9 or 10, or turning 18 and going pubbing and clubbing with real ID can be quite exhilarating. But remind them to take it easy and not go overboard. Moderation is key. And always look after each other.

PARTY

Pubbing and clubbing? Practise moderation

Alcohol impairs. Getting drunk distorts your ability to risk assess

Rohypnol: don't leave your drinks exposed

Think! Where are my friends? Are they safe?

You come together, you leave together. Make a plan and stick to it

Music Madness!

Both of us have lived in the UK for many years and agree the music festival scene here is quite impressive. In fact, it blows our proverbial wellies off! Allison is far more comfortable lost in the Glastonbury or Funk & Soul Weekender scenes than Deana. After surviving heavy rains and mudslides at Latitude a few years back, Deana has sworn never to return to festival-dom. There are more music festivals here than can be counted, hundreds of them, but the Big Daddy of them all remains Glastonbury. Measuring 900 acres, the site is massive. It is a small city of stages, tents, dance floors and food caravans teeming with a population of up to 180,000 people. Reading and Leeds, Latitude, V Festival, T in the Park, Camp Bestival and many others also sell out quickly thanks to their world-renowned headline acts and unrivalled music production standards. For visitors from around the world, the British set the standards for world-class music festivals like no other.

The average age of British ticket buyers for these massive outdoor concerts is 33 years old, according to Festivalawards. com. But tens of thousands of younger fans arrive en masse ready to let off some steam after studying for GCSE and A level exams. The age many teenagers first venture into the festival scene is post GCSE, so 16, and even more so post A levels: 17 or 18. They are young and ready to party, and the hedonistic atmosphere is naturally, or at times chemically, intoxicating. The bewitching combination of youth, music, alcohol and possibly drugs all adds up to a euphoric buzz. This in turn can induce sensible kids to throw caution to the wind ... And this is where

The RAP Project makes a point to discuss the top concerns that parents, and their teenagers, might have. Again, having delivered Music Festival Madness talks to many teenagers, they in turn feed back to us what teenagers going to festivals for the first time should consider. Here is what tops the list of what they are concerned about:

- Theft
- Alcohol/drugs
- Rape/sexual assault
- Violence
- Hydration
- Illness
- Weather
- Crowd control

We don't want to terrorise our teens with bad news stories but we do discuss what has happened in the past. These festivals are, for the most part, highly organised, very safe, extremely well run, professionally set up and promote a sense of camaraderie. We do describe to them two rapes that occurred at Latitude in 2010, as well as a fatal incident of crowd control at another festival abroad in Duisburg. This incident left 19 people dead. Allison, at Glastonbury in 2009, experienced a frightening incident while leaving the Pyramid Stage when Amy Winehouse finished her act and was replaced by Jay-Z. For what seemed an eternity, but may have lasted 45 minutes, thousands of people pushed against each other going in two different directions. The official crowd control patrol was not on hand, as far as she could see, and she felt the issue serious enough to take up with the founding farmer of the festival, Michael Eavis CBE, in an interview for ABC News in 2009. 'We have security in place to assist festival goers moving from one stage to another. Obviously, with such a big name, extra care has to be taken.' If your teen is new to the festival experience, please make them aware that crowds can be an issue and stress how important it is to stay calm in case of a crowd surge.

First off, your teenager should print off a map of the festival site before arriving. Large or small, knowing the lay of the land and the location of the First Aid tent, Lost and Found and the set up of stages, tents and loos is a good thing. We suggest they not imbibe en route to the festival as the queues are long to check in and receive wristbands, and they need their wits about them while they find a place to pitch their tent. Ensure they leave their valuables at home and say 'hello' to their neighbours at their temporary lodging. This simple gesture can create a sense of community and people are more likely to look out for you and your belongings. A bit of high-tech advice for your teen: tie a bell to the tent zip. This acts as a makeshift alarm system, alerting them to an unwelcome visitor. Also, we strongly recommend identifying a meeting place in case they lose their mates or their mobile phones. Phone reception can be poor, especially at the more rural locations, so it is a good idea to arrange a place to meet, say the falafel hut, at allotted times throughout the day and evening.

Sometimes someone may have to compromise on which act is seen or not seen in order to stick together. Negotiate, as things are more likely to go wrong if one is isolated. There are drugs at festivals and we have seen them randomly given out at crowded gigs. MDMA, cocaine, marijuana and legal highs are readily available. These can make our teenagers sick or even worse.

Regarding sexual assault, men and women should stick to public areas and stay on well-worn paths. If they are out of it and looking for the latrine in the middle of the night on their own, they can be led further afield. We recommend staying together, even going to the loo together if it is desolate and late at night. If anything should happen, medical attention should be sought immediately.

Again, having spoken to experienced festivalgoers and to teenagers who have been to a festival before, they have shared what to bring for the weekend:

THE RIGHT STUFF

- Tent
- Sleeping bag
- Wet wipes
- Money
- Bum bags
- Ear plugs
- Raincoat
- Wellies
- Sun cream
- Toiletries
- Condoms
- Torch
- Insect repellent
- Inexpensive watch
- Antiseptic wipes
- Plugless charger

These festivals are almost always amazing experiences, where teenagers bond with their friends, are exposed to top-notch music, funky silent discos and where memories are made. While their revelry is well-deserved, they should keep both dancing feet on the ground.

FESTIVAL

Flexibility: be prepared to compromise on which acts to see

Eat and drink plenty of water. Stay hydrated

Stay safe. If you get into trouble, find the medical tent or police

Tie a bell on your tent zip and make an alarm system

Indulge carefully: don't overdo it

Valuables. Leave the laptops and smartphones at home!

Arrange a meeting point in case you are separated

Look after each other and don't get isolated

TOP TIPS

- Find out if parents will be present or not at a party beforehand
- Look for your friends if you have not seen him or her for a while. Is she passed out somewhere? Is he sick?
- Stay hydrated and eat something
- Don't feel pressured to do anything you don't want to do
- If you are uncomfortable at a party, call home and ask for a lift back
- Get a map of the festival beforehand so you know the set up
- Enjoy the festival vibe, but don't overdo it

Resources

Alcohol Education Trust

www.alcoholeducationtrust.org

Chivalry is Sexy

#chivalryissexy

Drinkaware

www.drinkaware.co.uk

Festival Awards

www.festivalawards.com

Festival jobs

www.festaff.co.uk/volunteer-info
www.e4s.co.uk/jobs/1-summer-festival-jobs.htm

FRANK

www.talktofrank.com

Latitude

www.latitudefestival.com

NHS Festival personal safety guide

www.nhs.uk/Livewell/Festivalhealth/Pages/Safety.aspx

Reading

www.readingfestival.com

The Festival Calendar

www.thefestivalcalendar.co.uk

White Ribbon Campaign

www.whiteribboncampaign.co.uk

8 Mind the Gap: Travelling Safely Abroad

'Twenty years from now you will be more disappointed by the things that you didn't do than by the ones you did do. So throw off the bowlines. Sail away from the safe harbor. Catch the trade winds in your sails. Explore. Dream. Discover.'

Mark Twain

After A levels, many of our teenagers leave for either university or opt to take a gap year. After years of intense exams, putting off continuous education may well be the break many of them need and deserve. As adults, we envy them. With regards to either of the above, however, each is a leap into the unknown. This chapter addresses the practical and personal safety challenges faced by teens as they venture to exotic and far-flung places, and nails down the nitty-gritty of taking a year out. All teenagers' experiences will be different, but the practical elements and messages will normally be the same. The next chapter – The Big Leap – addresses the jump to university in detail.

There are many adventurous and creative ways for our teens to spend their gap year. For example, if your teen is interested in ecology and the great outdoors, there are animal care and conservation projects they could get involved with. Many of these opportunities will take them to places like Africa to help save endangered wildlife or to South America to help preserve the rainforest. If they enjoy working with children there are plenty of agencies placing students working as au pairs in another country, where children are encouraged to learn English not just at school but in their own homes. This is an excellent opportunity for your teenager to hone their foreign language skills. There are also cultural programmes allowing teens to teach drama, art or music to children from disadvantaged backgrounds. If they like being physical, they can work as a farmhand. If they are sporty, they can work as a ski instructor or teach football in India. They can also learn a foreign language or teach English. Some teens we know have taught in schools in Uganda, worked on archaeological digs in Greece, taught English in China, found work experience in New York or studied German in Berlin.

If your traveller is going to take advantage of one of the many opportunities offered by various organisations and companies, it is always best to get a recommendation from someone who has used them in the past. Many companies provide structured placements, orientation upon arrival, meals, accommodation and local 24-hour support. The amount of money these companies charge varies as do the services they provide. It is also best to get a recommendation from someone who has already gone on a gap year, ideally recently. If that is not possible, have the company provide you with a couple of references so you can perhaps contact someone who has used them in the past. Regardless what company you choose with your teen, at the very least make sure it complies with the British Standards Institution (BSI) and is certified by the Association of British Travel Agents (ABTA).

According to ABTA, approximately 25,000 students headed abroad for extended travel in 2015, and the top gap year destinations are:

1. Australia
2. New Zealand
3. USA

4. Peru
5. Vietnam
6. Thailand
7. Canada
8. Brazil
9. Argentina
10. India

Wherever they are thinking of going, most of the young people we know planning to take a gap year, or who have already completed their gap year, tend to work for several months at home first saving money to fund their adventure.

Let's face it, most gap year opportunities are not money-makers. So, when choosing what they want to do and where they want to go, your teen needs to budget carefully. As it is such a big decision they should also question what they want to accomplish. What skills do they want to develop? How will this experience enhance their future job prospects? It may be that a gap year for them is about developing independence or it may be that they want to test whether they want to work in a particular career, like conservation or teaching. Regardless, they need to plan it out carefully.

There are many considerations when helping your teen choose where to go on their gap year, but one concern as parents is their health and safety. Reading the news, it doesn't take long to find gap year horror stories: young people are robbed, sexually assaulted or even worse. At The RAP Project, we have been told some pretty crazy gap year stories. The daughter of a good friend of ours, Kirsty, was doing a conservation placement in Madagascar. She would Skype her mum from an Internet cafe that she had to walk about three miles to get to from the village where she was living. She described the beauty of the beach she was living on, the most magnificent sunsets and the hospitality of the villagers. There were many other volunteers like herself, students from all over the world taking time out from their studies to participate in this unique opportunity. One evening, however, all of the foreign students were rounded up by the local villagers and ushered into the local bar in town. They were barricaded in, told to remain quiet and not to leave the building. The villagers informed them that they were tipped off that the town was going to be raided by 'bandits'. These raids happened periodically and the purpose was to rob the villagers. In the past some people had been hurt. Kirsty was understandably terrified. The village was raided as warned, no one was hurt and none of the foreign students' belongings were stolen. Kirsty continued her work in Madagascar and loved her time spent there. The raid was a very small part of what was an otherwise wonderful experience.

However, sometimes stories don't have a happy ending. In 2013 two 18-year-old girls from London suffered atrocious injuries when they had battery acid thrown at them by two men on a moped in Zanzibar. Both girls had just finished a programme where they were teaching English to underprivileged children. They immediately returned to London to seek medical treatment. As of today the perpetrators have not been brought to justice and there has been no explanation offered for why they were attacked. A young man we know was travelling in India on his gap year. He had bought a bottle of water as he was advised to do when he was travelling. After drinking the water, he passed out. When he woke up, he had been robbed. His money and valuables were gone and he has no memory of what happened. The water had been tampered with, most likely with Rohypnol or a similar drug. Another woman we spoke to was told to avoid bottled water while travelling around China. Branded cans of Coke or Sprite were suggested in favour of bottles of water, which were more easily tampered with. This is not to say your teen should avoid drinking water while travelling, but remind them to remain vigilant about its source.

Other students have told us stories of young women being targeted for sexual attacks while travelling abroad. At a resort in Cyprus, a girl was drugged after she snogged a local man who slipped a pill in her mouth while kissing. She was completely unaware of what had happened to her. Young women also told us that they were warned to be wary of men in vans pretending to be emergency medical workers. They would park near bars and clubs and if a young woman was taken ill from alcohol consumption they would 'collect' her and sexually assault her. We asked the girls who told us about these incidents how it affected their travel plans. They said that, though it didn't affect their decision to travel, they were super diligent about looking after one another. They did not go off with anyone they met on their trip and they did not leave their drinks unattended or travel on their own. They enjoyed their trip and returned home with a suitcase of great memories.

It is essential that our kids know, understand and respect the cultural norms of the countries they are visiting. On 30 May 2015, 23-year-old Briton, Eleanor Hawkins, along with three other travellers, was arrested and jailed in Malaysia for 'committing an obscene act in public'. Eleanor posed topless on top of Mount Kinabalu, which is considered sacred ground by the local population. The young travellers' antics outraged many Malaysian people and hence led to criminal prosecution. In court the lawyer representing the group claimed that the foreign defendants were unaware of local customs. Though what they did would be of little consequence, say, in the south of France, it caused a huge controversy in Malaysia.

The downside to our digital natives going abroad is that the Internet spreads generalisations and unfortunate incidents faster, and subsequently more convincingly, than ever. Britons abroad have been stereotyped at one time or another as sunburned, football loving, Union Jack wearing, drunken louts. The unfortunate incident of a young woman who was filmed performing oral sex on 24 men during a pub crawl in Magaluf, Mallorca in July 2014 didn't help matters. The video went viral within minutes, thus cementing the pub, its landlord and the drunken 18-year-old's reputation in cyberspace forever. Regarding buying, selling, importing or exporting drugs, we always mention the laws in Turkey and Malaysia, as they are particularly strict. One 16-year-old girl we know went on holiday with her family and a friend. The two girls walked down to the market and stopped to admire some fruit. The salesman approached them and whispered 'pot, pot' and offered them a baggie to buy. Sarah took the baggie, opened it and smelled it. She then gave it back to him and moved on as she didn't want any. According to the US Embassy in Turkey's website, penalties for violating Turkish laws, even unknowingly, can be severe. Penalties for possession, use, or trafficking in illegal drugs in Turkey are particularly strict, and convicted offenders should expect jail sentences with heavy fines. If Sarah had been spotted by a policeman carrying this baggie, even though only for a second, she could have faced 4–10 years of imprisonment according to Turkish law. We are sure our kids will never have heard of the film 'Midnight Express', but we certainly remember it well. Maybe organise a screening before they set off? Over in Southeast Asia, Malaysia and Singapore have the toughest drug laws on the planet, according to Goseasia.about.com. If you are caught carrying a gram of heroin or cocaine, you could spend two to five years in jail plus receive a painful beating with a rattan whip. If someone is caught with 14 grams of heroin or 40 grams of cocaine, he or she can expect the death penalty. If whippings don't scare, warn them of arbitrary but mandatory drug testing. Anyone under the mere suspicion of illegal drug taking can be held without warrant for up to 15 days, no questions asked. For all the reasons above, don't buy or sell drugs abroad, or at home for that matter. And remind your traveller not to carry anything for anyone any under circumstances. If they are caught carrying drugs, even unbeknownst to them, they are criminally liable.

These are the worse case scenarios and, of course, the polar opposite stereotype of a Briton abroad on a gap year is the posh young person who is 'roughing it' in lovely hotels, not hostels, and living comparatively grandly off a parental allowance rather than having to get down and dirty and earn his or her keep. Oxford graduate and comedian Matt Lacey created a rather well heeled 'Gap Yah' alter ego, known as Orlando Charmon, and posted his sketches on YouTube. With over 5 million viewers, he has been accused of spreading negative perceptions of young Britons on the road far from home.

The point is that we can't help but worry that false stereotyping could possibly lead to dangerous assumptions. We can't help but think again of the 2015 New Year's sexual assaults that took place in Europe. These attacks were clearly planned in Germany, Switzerland, Sweden and Austria. Were they planned on social media? Germany's Federal Minister of Justice Heiko Maas called the crimes a 'new dimension'. Obviously, The RAP Project promotes the gap year experience as a positive, exciting opportunity but, with the digital age, maybe teenagers should consider the pros and cons of keeping a low profile, practising discretion and avoiding massive crowds. It is certainly worth a conversation, in any case. For example, we never lecture young people on how to dress while they are living here in UK – whether someone chooses to wear tight jeans or a short skirt is their prerogative and not an indication of their sexual availability. However, if our young traveller is in Calcutta or Mumbai should they wear the same outfit as they would if they were going clubbing in Soho? Probably not. And whether it is out of cultural respect or safety concerns, it is essential for our young adventurer to try to 'blend in' as much as possible. Should they open up a map in a bar in Rio and loudly point out where their hotel may be located? Again, probably not.

Travelling in the Digital Age

The positive aspect of travelling in the digital age is that all of the information your teen needs is readily available online and able to be downloaded in apps. Nowadays, the bureaucracy of researching trips, from continents to the tiniest of hamlets, is almost null and void. Why cart heavy Lonely Planets around in your rucksack when its seasoned publisher has one of the best travel websites around? From details on the best beaches and cultural treasures to visa requirements and up-to-date warnings on where to avoid from the UK's Foreign & Commonwealth Office, as well as travellers sharing information on its Thorn Tree forum and so much more, it is an enormous resource.

The ability to compare the best prices for trains, buses and planes online is now a hobby for many young people. Once in a universe not so far away, travel agents ruled the roost in expert travel advice, but now everyone can access booking sites such as Expedia.co.uk, Momondo.co.uk, Skyscanner.net and Kayak. co.uk, among many, and trawl through a bundle of flights to find the best price, route and dates. It is important that your teen books a return flexible ticket in advance as well as their first night or more of accommodation in the city or country they are first visiting. Travellers can also enjoy the benefits of online and mobile check-in, and travelling light will cut out baggage fees as well as ensure quicker mobility through train, bus or airport terminals. Despite all the benefits of the digital age, however, we would advise all travellers, at any age, to pack maps, as this may be one necessity you could not do without if WiFi is not available.

Perhaps the greatest development from a parental perspective has been the birth of VoIP, or Voice over Internet Protocol. Yes, we Googled this so you wouldn't have to! VoIP is a form of technology that allows for speech communication via the Internet. Skype and Viber remain popular, but FaceTime and WhatsApp are also being used more and more. Download these apps and make sure your kids do too before they head off, and say farewell to postcards in the post. Installing Skype and Viber is a pretty straightforward process, however both apps work differently. Skype needs a sign up with a username and password, while Viber only requires your phone number (it also needs a username but only as a number identifier), and both, of course, require WiFi. We tend to use Skype in our households as we can schedule a voice and video call – a great way to catch up with family or friends abroad – but Viber has one massive edge, in our opinion in that it works better on hand-held devices (saving your traveller carrying a laptop around). Hopefully, young people abroad are not spending their entire time on their laptops opting instead for life-changing, cultural, personal, horizon-enhancing experiences. Skype works only if you are online and logged on to the app. In contrast, if you are connected to the Internet, Viber will ring on the phone. Before your child leaves, they should give you a comprehensive itinerary of their travels. And if their plans change, as they often do, they can easily keep you up-to-date and informed.

Here is a list of the most popular gap year travel apps:

- **Google Translate**: translates words and phrases either by text or pronunciation
- **Google Maps/Google Street View**: know your location and the lay of the land
- **XE Currency Converter**
- **WiFi Finder**: keep data roaming off and find your nearest WiFi hotspot
- **TripIt**: keeps track of elaborate travel plans and documents. Enables you to create a master itinerary
- **TravelSafe**: shares a huge database of common emergency numbers to carry with you, all available without an Internet connection

- **skyScanner**: finds the best airfares
- **Google Goggles:** take a picture, upload it and Google will do its best to identify the object, place or text (Android phone only)
- **HostelBookers**: book great value hostels and cheap hotels
- **Lonely Planet**: packed with tips and advice from on-the-ground experts, its city guides are a fantastic resource

As our teens have grown up in the digital age, they are susceptible to using the Internet as a security blanket. With the Internet so prominent around the world, anyone, young or old, is tempted to log in to favoured news websites, video downloads or Netflix accounts. For those of you who take their jobs on the road, how many of you have actually chosen a digital detox over the WiFi code as soon as you arrive on holiday? Allison's family has certainly adapted its work habits to the extent that a holiday without WiFi is not possible, so accustomed are workaholic family members to working and resting while on holiday. Can any of us today really live offline, off grid and let go? We hope so. Why not encourage your children before they hit the road to reconnect with the world and its people offline while they travel abroad? The Internet is handy for practical purposes, but nothing beats real life adventure.

Health and Safety

Travel insurance

Take out a comprehensive medical and travel insurance policy for your child. Even if they are staying in Europe to travel and have a European Health Insurance Card (EHIC), you may need to take out additional coverage. The European Health Insurance

Card, for example, limits coverage to reduced or limited emergency care coverage. There are various policies available with various coverage options, so please read the fine print. At the bare minimum the policy should cover personal liability and damage, not only for the policyholder but for people or property they cause damage or harm to. Coverage for personal property, such as passports or tickets, as well as coverage for legal costs that can be accrued while travelling abroad are additional options you may want to consider. It's also important to check the policy's cancellation conditions. If, for example, your child visits a country that the Foreign & Commonwealth Office advises against travelling to, this may negate the policy's coverage if an incident occurs while visiting that country.

When your traveller heads abroad, they should have the name of their insurance company with international emergency numbers written down somewhere safe as well as their policy number. If something criminal or accidental occurs when they are travelling, they need to report the crime before they depart the country in which it occurred. The point of this is twofold. First, in terms of criminal incidents, law enforcement will probably not take any criminal action unless the report is filed contemporaneous to the incident. Second, for insurance purposes, financial reimbursement for lost or stolen property will not happen unless the insurance claim is accompanied by a police report. For young women, if they are a victim of a crime, sexual or otherwise, they should request a female police officer and/or doctor. We advise this as it is for their own protection, although we recognise that this may not always be a realistic option.

Jabs and medicine

Ensure that your traveller has all the necessary jabs that are required for countries they are visiting. If their travels are to exotic far-off places, it is crucial they get vaccinated before they leave the UK. Please note that many of the jabs required need to be done within a certain time frame for them to be effective. It is recommended that your traveller see their healthcare provider 6–8 weeks before they travel to receive the vaccinations that are required. Also, when your traveller is providing information to their healthcare provider about where they are intending to go, it is important that they are as specific as possible not only about the countries they are travelling to, but *where* in the country they will be visiting and what activities they may undertake. For example, if they are travelling to Thailand and only going to Bangkok, it is recommended that they have a tetanus and a hepatitis B jab. However, if they are going trekking to more rural areas additional jabs are recommended, such as hepatitis A and rabies. The NHS website provides a very compressive list of required vaccinations required while travelling abroad.

It is essential, too, that your traveller pays a final visit to their GP before heading off. If they require prescription medication, have them take enough to last them for their journey. The medication should be kept in its original packaging and carried in their hand luggage in case their main backpack or suitcase is lost or delayed while travelling. It's also a good idea to check whether their prescription medication, as well as any over-the-counter medication they may be carrying, is legal in the countries they are visiting.

FIRST AID KIT

There are countless first aid kits available to suit your teen's needs and budget, and they are essential when travelling abroad. Depending on where they are travelling, they may need insect wipes, diarrhoea relief and/or water purification tablets. Research has taught us that lightweight, compact, waterproof first aid kits are best.

Passports and Visas

Though it may sound patronising, make sure your traveller's passport has at least six months left before it expires prior to their departure. Many countries will not allow entry if there is less than a six-month validation period remaining on a visitor's passport.

A passport may not be sufficient to gain entry into certain countries. If they need a visa, note that requirements may vary. For example, entry into Russia requires that UK citizens provide fingerprints and the negative results of an HIV test to the Russian embassy in order to obtain a visa for visitation. As of 2015, Kenya now requires an electronic visa to be obtained before port of entry. You'll find some suggested websites which provide support for these types of logistics at the end of this chapter (page 178).

Two copies of passports and visas should be made: one to be kept in a safe place at home with a family member in case the original is lost or stolen while travelling, and the other kept with the traveller and stored separately from the original documents. Your traveller should also take with them a second form of photo ID, for example a driving licence, a learner's driving licence or student ID.

Cash, Credit Cards and Currency

It is hard to judge how much money your child will need on their travels. Much of it is dependent upon where they are going and for how long they are going to be abroad. They should plan a budget before they leave which allows for unexpected expenses, such as changing travel tickets or for booking day trips they hadn't originally planned. Tell your travellers to try and stick to their budget as best they can. Luckily, as opposed to when we were travelling as students,

ATM hole in the wall 24-hour access to cash is readily available, easing your mind while they are away in terms of your teen's financial security.

Although cash is king as they say, your traveller should diversify their portfolio. They should have one debit card, one credit card, some currency and some traveller's cheques. Make sure that both the credit card company and the bank who issued the cards are informed of their travel plans. Many banks and credit card companies will block cards for suspected fraud if a purchase is made abroad and they are not informed of the cardholder's travel plans in advance. Your child should write down the emergency number for the bank and/or credit card company, as well as their account numbers, in case their cards are lost or stolen. And though not always fashionable, for safety purposes, they should wear a money belt hidden beneath their clothes for carrying valuables, travel documents and money. Some people find it convenient to download their bank's app, allowing them to keep up-to-date with their bank balance while abroad.

Packing It All In

Packing at the best of times can be a challenging exercise, but when going off on a gap year to what can be countries with very different climates, terrains and topography, it can seem overwhelming to your adventurer ... and to you as their parent. So here is a basic list of some essentials:

- First aid kit with insect repellent and sterile needle kit
- Prescription medication and inhaler (if needed)
- Wet wipes
- Alcohol wipes
- Mosquito netting
- Sleeping bag and sleeping bag liner
- Money belt

- Day rucksack
- Two padlocks: one small one for the rucksack; one large one for the door
- Personal safety alarm
- Sunblock
- Portable charger
- Worldwide adapter
- LED hand torch and head torch
- Water bottle
- Water purification tablets
- Contraception
- Maps

With this information, your kids will hopefully enjoy a well-planned trip with access to resources which can enhance their experience as well as help them cope with last minute changes. Lucky them. We wish we could go on a gap year ourselves!

GAP YEAR

Gather relevant cultural and social information. Know the local customs

Avoid travelling alone, walking alone or eye contact in certain countries

Plan your trip well and leave behind a detailed itinerary

You must be aware of the risks involved unique to the places you are visiting

Embassy information: know your consulate's phone number and location

Avoid attracting attention and try to blend in as much as possible

Report a criminal incident before you leave the country and request a female police officer and/or a female doctor

TOP TIPS

- Use the apps
- If you need to work during your travels, try to line it up beforehand. There are plenty of English language jobs to be found
- Always book your first night of accommodation
- Bring local currency as well as a credit card, debit card and traveller's cheques
- Respect local culture: be sensitive to what might offend
- Don't transport packages for anyone else but yourself
- Enjoy your adventure but don't take unnecessary risks

Resources

Expedia

www.expedia.co.uk

GapGuru

www.gapguru.com/GapYearPlanning/Visas-And-Vaccination

Gap year advice

http://gapadvice.org/

Gap year visas

www.gapyear.com/plan/visas

GOV.UK travel advice

www.gov.uk/foreign-travel-advice
www.gov.uk/guidance/gap-year-foreign-travel-advice

KAYAK

www.kayak.co.uk

Lonely Planet

www.lonelyplanet.com/

momondo

www.momondo.co.uk/

NHS travel vaccinations

www.nhs.uk/conditions/Travel-immunisation/Pages/Introduction.aspx

skyscanner

www.skyscanner.net

Year out group

www.yearoutgroup.org/

9 The Big Leap

'University's like this little world, a bubble of time separate from everything before and everything after.'

Mhairi McFarlane

Arriving at university for the first time is similar to jumping off a high dive in free fall. You know your child is going to hit the water eventually, but will he effortlessly glide into the water or belly flop in pain? Either way, our freshers are going to feel the shock. The dramatic departure from home to university is so often underestimated that we were asked to design a RAP Project presentation specifically on this transition, which we entitled 'The Big Leap'. As McFarlane observes in the above quote, life now will be very much measured by 'before' and 'after'. Suddenly our teenagers have their first taste of freedom, but is it pure nectar or pure terror? They will have no one to wake them up in the morning, to shout at them to tidy their room or demand what time to be home on a Saturday night. Suddenly, major life decisions once made by parents will now be made by these young adults. Will they find this invigorating, exciting or overwhelming?

When we deliver our Big Leap talk to sixth form students we are very aware of the heavy pressures they are under. Not only are they wrestling with course selection, university visits and UCAS application forms, they are struggling to achieve As and A*s in their exams. The Headmasters' and Headmistresses' Conference (HMC), representing some 65 independent schools, released data from its first survey on national teenage mental health concerns in October 2015. Chris Jeffery, Chair of the HMC's Wellbeing Working Group, said, 'Young people in all types of school are experiencing pressures like never before. They worry about getting the right grades in public exams that appear ever more important, a place at their chosen university and a good career beyond that so they can pay off increasing levels of student debt – all whilst constantly trying to look their best on social media.' So with the exams and selection process now behind them, many young adults feel a justified sense of achievement. A friend's 18-year-old son was so relieved he survived his A level exams that he could barely move afterwards and spent most of the next few weeks sleeping and eating. When his parents had the audacity to suggest a summer job, he glared and said, 'You are kidding me?' A little aggro, perhaps, but we firmly believe parents cannot overestimate the pressure our teens face during this crucial time.

With the autumn chill and Freshers' Week around the corner, our university-bound kids are leaving their safe circle of friends, family and routine behind for the unknown at a much larger, less personal institution. In our Big Leap presentation, we ask sixth form students what they look forward to most about leaving school for uni, as well as what they feel most vulnerable about. Here's what they say:

- Independence
- Excitement
- Freedom
- Alcohol
- Fear
- Sexual experience
- Sense of the unknown

We find the well-known 'W Curve', developed by William Zeller and Robert Mosier in 1993, accurately reflects the settling in period and adjustment of a first year student at university. Though this illustration may not reflect everyone's experience at the same time, we believe it is a good guide to the roller coaster of emotions that many first year students experience.

When a student turns up at university, there is clearly an initial 'honeymoon' period that is experienced upon arrival, encompassing the elation of freedom, the right to decide what time to wake up in the morning, which classes to attend, as well as what and when to eat. But, as the old adage says, 'What goes up must come down.' This is the 'cultural shock' phase. Normally within the first couple of months, students are hit with the reality of university life. They are trying to fit in with a new circle of friends, learning how to budget money and staying on top of their workload without the same deadlines and discipline from a form teacher breathing down their necks. The 'initial adjustment' period begins when they really begin to settle in. They have taken on the practical responsibility of registering with a local GP, discovered a hair salon or barber, a favourite pub and some mates. With these accomplishments under their belt, they begin to feel much more comfortable.

According to the designers of this graph, students then enter a phase called 'mental isolation' when the first term is over and they return home for the Christmas holidays. This 'mental isolation' describes the feelings of being caught between two worlds, having moved on from home and their secondary school friends but not yet rooted to the new life at university. They don't really fit into either place, often experiencing isolation and detachment. This can be a very lonely time for kids. As parents we need to look out for their emotional well-being when they are home for the holidays. In an attempt to prove to us that they are now adults, our first year university students back home may hide their vulnerabilities. It really is a major academic, logistic and emotional chasm they are crossing, and it is worth chatting quietly with them about the good and the bad aspects of their new life before they return.

Hopefully, upon returning to uni after a long break, there is what the 'W' authors describe as a new-found feeling of 'acceptance & integration'. Students are now more optimistic about their evolving university life and friendships, and return to a more familiar rhythm.

Drinking

There are two words that have instilled worry and concern in many parents' minds: 'Freshers' Week'. You can hardly open a newspaper in late August and September without being bombarded with stories about the alcohol-fuelled, misogynistic, bacchanalian romps awaiting your 18-year-old children. There are elements of truth to some of this but, for the most part, the first week at university is normally set up by the students' union to introduce freshers to new places, new faces and to help them familiarise themselves with the layout of the university. And most university websites now advertise alcohol-free mixers and socials alongside the more stereotypical booze-fuelled events.

Unlike at school, where some people can legally drink and others are not yet 18, the majority of students can drink when they reach university and, quite frankly, alcohol can serve as a successful social lubricant during Freshers' Week. Of course, a good many choose not to imbibe, but a good many will, and many will more than likely overdo it at least once. Why? Well, they are in a new environment, with people they do not know. For many young people, consuming alcohol in a shared communal environment will empower them, rightly or wrongly, to feel more confident socially, and therefore more relaxed to chat, dance, flirt, etc.

But now, more than ever, when they have yet to really establish trusting relationships or understand their physical environment, it is crucial for teens to remember a few golden rules. Ask your kids before sending them off to practise self-awareness around alcohol and understand how their body absorbs alcohol. Do they undergo a radical personality change when they drink? Do they blackout or do they manage to alternate water with wine? Can they clearly communicate if they are drunk? Can they give consent if necessary? Stress the importance of going out with a buddy and coming home with a buddy. Oh yeah, and *eat something.*

This is a story told by Imogen, a fresher at university. Having always been quite sheltered and well behaved throughout school, she saw uni as an opportunity to reinvent herself. The day arrived when her parents nervously moved her things into her halls and said 'Goodbye'. Imogen no sooner left her unpacked bags, flew out the door and checked out the noticeboards and parties on offer during Freshers' Week. To her delight, a friendly and lively group of girls from the halls decided that they would attend some of the parties together and look out for each other. On her very first night, she met this attractive young man named Michael. They were actually from the same region in the northeast and knew some people in common. They exchanged phone numbers and ended up arranging to meet up at the end of the week.

Imogen was never a drinker throughout secondary school, and often on a diet. She had learned from her schoolmates, her mother and the fashion magazines that avoiding carbohydrates was *the* way to keep thin. Like most young women, Imogen felt self-conscious about her appearance and weight. Skipping dinner to feel more confident, she arranged to meet Michael at a local pub. Nervous, she noticed once again how cute Michael was. 'Too cute for me,' she thought. She downed a couple of glasses of wine to calm her nerves. The conversation flowed, and one glass of wine followed another. She didn't stop to think about eating something or drinking a glass of water. At some point late in the evening, after stumbling and slurring, Michael suggested they leave. As they went outside, Imogen fell over and vomited into a bush. Michael helped her up and brought her safely back to her room. Fortunately, this new friend really looked after her and made sure she was safe. He made the effort to track down her roommate in case she was sick again. Having been in a very vulnerable situation, Imogen was lucky Michael acted responsibly and with kindness. We always tell the students that 'Chivalry is Sexy'. More often than not they ask us what 'chivalry' means, and we give them this modernised take on it, explaining that it is when male or female friends look after one another.

Sexual Assault

There is a direct correlation between alcohol and sexual assaults or rape at university. The Office for National Statistics and the Institute of Alcohol Studies have both done much research on this, and there is no doubt that alcohol is a date rape drug along with Rohypnol. Drinking and drug taking impairs one's ability to communicate to want to go home, to make clear decisions, to assess risky situations, to say 'Stop', to consent or to defend yourself from an attack. It is just common sense. And that is what needs to be empha- sised to your child.

We believe that discussing alcohol consumption or experi- menting with drugs and how it can influence behaviour is important. We do not have to support, agree or respect our kids' choices, and we certainly do not intend in any way to judge someone's alcohol consumption or their correlative behaviour, but we do worry about our teenagers at university putting themselves in a vulnerable situation without a familiar safety net.

Millie arrived for her first year at university with all of the optimism a parent could hope for. Despite the large urban setting, Millie quickly acclimatised to university life, joined plenty of clubs and made good friends. In her halls, there was a mixture of friendly first and second year students, with the second year students often taking the first years under their wing. Not surprisingly, romances blossomed. Millie's roommate Karen started dating a second year student, Tom, who lived down the hall. The three of them would often hang out together, go to parties, the pub and have a good time. Tom was always around and became a sort of big brother to Millie. Before Easter break, Karen and Tom broke up. Karen, like most other students, left to go home for the holiday. Millie stayed on for a few more days to finalise a paper. One night she and some friends went to the pub before everyone headed back home. Tom joined them. Everyone was relaxed and in a good mood, but Millie remembers most people were tired and wanted an early night. Millie left the pub with a friend and they walked back to their halls.

Millie arrived back at her room, locked the door behind her and went to bed. She fell asleep immediately. But to her horror, she woke up in the middle of the night with Tom on top of her. He was sexually assaulting her. In the early morning daylight, she found Tom asleep on Karen's bed. Confused, Millie did not know what to do next. As with many victims, she felt dirty and wanted to wash everything away, including the disturbing memory of what had happened. She took a long, hot shower and wept. She quietly got dressed and slipped out of the door and ran to her friend Amanda's room. Deeply concerned over Millie's well-being, Amanda escorted her to see Jo, the hall's senior resident, to report what had happened. Jo calmly listened to Millie's story. After expressing sympathy, she explained that as the university was essentially shut down for the break, there were no other officials to report this to. She advised Millie to head home, have a good rest and that they would confront the situation when school resumed in a few weeks. Millie, still reeling from the emotional and physical repercussions of what Tom had done to her, numbly agreed and followed Jo's misguided advice.

At home, Millie withdrew from her family and old friends. Her parents just assumed that she was tired from exams. Millie lived the next few weeks in a fog, not knowing what to do or who to turn to for help. She couldn't comprehend why Tom, someone she trusted and looked up to, could do what he did to her. She didn't understand why Jo, the senior resident, whose role was to guide students, suggested that she go home and get some rest, as if what happened to her was a trivial occurrence, like getting a low exam result that would be put in a better perspective after a good night's sleep. She reluctantly returned to university, still in a daze. Nothing looked the same to her and she felt like an outsider. Her world had changed. The university she so adored just weeks earlier now felt alien and unfamiliar.

Amanda encouraged Millie to speak to Jo again. Millie felt compelled to do something, file a report, see a counsellor, see a doctor ... Something. Amanda accompanied her to meet with Jo who informed them that she had spoken to Tom. He had admitted to what happened and said that he was very remorseful for what he had done to Millie. He wanted to meet with her to 'talk it over'. Jo encouraged Millie to meet with Tom. She said that he was truly sorry and that she did not think it would be 'fair' that Tom's life would be ruined for a mistake that he regrets. Jo assured her that the meeting would take place in a neutral place, her room, not either of theirs. She also assured Millie that she would be right outside of the room where the meeting took place so that Millie would feel 'safe'. Millie agreed to the meeting because, like many victims, she felt guilty and she didn't want to 'ruin' anyone's life. She had questions she wanted answered that she felt only Tom could. She thought maybe this meeting would provide closure.

She walked into Jo's dimly lit room and found Tom standing on the other side behind a desk. He approached her, put his arms around her and said, 'I am sorry.' Millie was immobile.

She was speechless, emotionless. Millie moved away from him and simply asked him how he had got into her room that night. Tom told her that Karen had given him a spare key that she had made for him when they were dating. He hadn't planned on doing what he did, he said, it just happened.

Millie spent the rest of the academic year aimlessly going from lecture to lecture. She could not concentrate and was unable to complete her exams. It was then that she reported what happened to the university. She was persuaded not to file formal charges against Tom by a university official. She was told that what happened was a 'misunderstanding' and because she had been drinking before the 'misunderstanding' her integrity would also be called into question. The university would not penalise her for what happened academically. Because she was unable to take her end of year exams, her transcript would reflect that a personal tragedy had occurred and therefore she was unable to complete the year. The report she filed on the incident was sealed, and would only be opened if an incident involving Tom occurred again. Millie transferred to a different university but spent the next three years going to counselling and trying to restore her sense of self and regain her former strength.

When she began uni, Millie was very trusting. She regrets not finding out who had a spare set of keys to their room. Of course, there is no guarantee that what happened to Millie would not have occurred anyway, albeit in a different way and under different circumstances. In hindsight, Millie wishes that she had spoken to her parents after the assault when she was home on break. They would have advised her on what to do and supported her emotionally. Millie, despite having a close relationship with her parents, felt that if she told them what happened, she would be letting them down. Aside from feeling that she was somehow to blame for what happened to her, she also wanted to prove to her parents that she was independent, infallible and perfectly capable of managing on her own. If she told them about the sexual assault, she really believed they would think less of her. When her parents did eventually find out, they were distraught about what their dear daughter had been put through, but also the fact that she didn't feel she could openly talk to them about this life-altering incident.

Unlike Imogen, Millie's story did not end well. We have heard from young women and young men who describe feelings of overwhelming shame and guilt in cases of rape and sexual assault. Fear of upsetting mum and dad, disappointing them, causing them pain or inspiring a murderous, vengeful plot against the assailant prevent many from initially telling their parents what happened. Our children, now young adults at university, do not want to let us down and can sometimes be afraid to open up to us. We send our children off to university with the hope that they will come back well-educated, independent adults ready to conquer the world. We also want them to stay safe and if something unforeseen does happen, as it did in Millie's case, we would expect a university to deal with it in an appropriate manner. There are programmes at some universities offering mandatory, consent classes and there are also some free online courses, but there is not, as of yet, a uniform, cohesive rulebook on how to counsel victims and punish assailants at universities. Based on our research, every university stateside and in the UK handles issues of sexual assault differently.

In January 2016, The RAP Project attended the Public Policy Exchange's (PPE) symposium, 'Tackling Rape, Sexual Assault and Harassment at Universities and Colleges'. One of the speakers, Lisa Benjamin, of the Somerset & Avon Rape & Sexual Abuse Support (SARSAS), spoke eloquently about the need for a coordinated campaign in dealing with sexual violence at universities. 'There must be a multi-agency approach to these incidents, which include the police, the local authority, the university, Rape Crisis and SARCS (sexual assault referral centres)'. This alternative is more palatable to the victim and their families, as it offers emotional support and legal guidance. Some universities refuse to investigate allegations of indecent assault or rape, believing that it is purely a police matter.

As we write this, Jon Krakauer's book *Missoula: Rape and the Justice System in a College Town* spends yet another week on the *New York Times* bestseller list. It is the first time a writer has investigated the vastly under-reported crime of acquaintance rape, now the most under-reported crime in America. Krakauer tackles the spate of sexual assaults on the Missoula campus at the University of Montana between 2008 and 2012. The university's administration came under national scrutiny for its failure to properly respond to these attacks. The result of this bestseller is that author Krakauer has greatly added momentum to the dialogue on campus rape as well as how these crimes are subsequently handled in the USA and here in the UK.

Back home, a 2013 report issued by the Ministry of Justice, the Home Office and the Office for National Statistics found that, 'female students in full-time education are at higher risk of sexual violence than the general female population'. National newspapers have been picking up on this story, namely the *Guardian* and the *Daily Telegraph*. The *Telegraph* contracted YouthSight, a specialist research group, to canvass 1,000 students across Britain in January 2015. The poll showed that a third of female students experienced a sexual assault or unwanted advances at university, and one in eight male students had also been subjected to groping or unwanted advances. Of the students polled 1 per cent of either gender said they had been raped at university. While these numbers are high, the poll concluded an equally shocking statistic: almost half (43 per cent) of those women who had experienced sexual assault, did not report their ordeal, even to friends or family. Six out of ten male victims also said they had not told anyone. Why is this? The victims said they did not think academic authorities would actually do anything about these incidents, so why bother? Those polled expressed very little trust in the system.

At about the same time, an alliance of charities and campaign groups created the End Violence Against Women (EVAW) coalition to look into exactly what policies were in place at UK universities. Its findings were bleak. The EVAW coalition concluded that higher education institutions did not have proper rape and harassment policies in place, and suggested that universities were shunning legal responsibilities by refusing to investigate sexual assault allegations.

An American postgraduate student at the University of Oxford alleges she was raped by a fellow student in 2011. Elizabeth Ramey reported the incident to the police but her assailant was not prosecuted due to a lack of evidence. She did not want her assailant to walk away free, however, and pursued a claim through the university's complaints board. Ramey charges that Oxford did not take the investigation seriously and, in a groundbreaking case, took the university to court over what she felt was a clear lack of policy. The University of Oxford, she alleged, condones a policy and procedure allowing them to avoid investigating allegations of serious sexual assault. The Equality and Human Rights Commission supported her argument; however the High Court judge did not. Ramey lost her case but the story generated a lot of media attention.

Unfortunately, there are numerous cases of rape at universities, from Aberdeen to Sussex. Ramey's experience is not a unique one. As a result, the NUS spearheaded a study called the NUS 'Lad Culture' audit between December 2014 and February 2015. Looking at 35 institutions and student unions, it concluded that there was a 'startling lack' of provision, training and support for victims of sexual violence and harassment. Only 51 per cent of the universities had a formal policy on sexual harassment, while the victims of sexual assault said they were not given appropriate or suitable guidance. Rape victims complained that they felt responsible for resolving the matter and at times were placed in the room with the perpetrator to mediate, just as Millie was. This is neither effective nor healthy and can further exacerbate difficult and painful emotions.

Men and women who experience this horrific crime should be given as much support as possible and certainly not be made to endure a system that works against them. We strongly believe in a mandatory systematic procedure that is followed by all universities and colleges in the UK. This makes so much sense to us. But why is there such reluctance to implement national guidelines? Are universities afraid of negative publicity? Are the victims not taken seriously or believed? Or is there a deep-rooted misogyny within higher education today?

Laddism

We cannot write this chapter without referencing what The Rap Project calls 'Lad-itude', the widespread phenomenon at universities throughout the country. Heads of pastoral care at the schools we visit ask us to specifically address it, as do the female students. We endeavour to curtail this behaviour, but it is an uphill battle. So, what do we mean by 'Laddism' and 'Lad-itude'?

According to the NUS, it is used to describe a 'subset of student culture that promotes a masculinity expressed through drinking to excess, playing certain manly sports, engaging in politically incorrect banter'. The banter is often sexist, misogynist and homophobic. Websites such as UNILAD and The LADbible are promoting this unattractive behaviour. We, like many organisations, cannot help but ask if this lad culture is playing a role in the rise of sexual assault and sexual harassment on university campuses. The following stories should be accompanied with a 'Warning: The Following Contains Shocking Content', but here we go...

When we began compiling information to create The RAP Project's Big Leap presentation for sixth formers, we again returned to the story of the Pembroke College rugby club. Remember the rugby club social secretary who sent an email to his 50 or so teammates with the subject line: 'Free Pussy'? Within the content of the email, the author encouraged them to seek out a fresher for an upcoming event. Their 'challenge' was to bring two bottles, one of which should be opened in advance and to 'include a substance of their choice'. The team were advised to be 'as clandestine as possible in their deed' and requested at least one player to 'bring a positive pregnancy test'.

The email, penned by Woo Kim, caused a furore. Mr Kim had to resign from his position, the social event was cancelled and the team subsequently attended a session on sexual consent. Talk about a slap on the wrist. If a person emailed a group of friends with the subject line 'Burglarising Old People' with instructions on targeting the homes of vulnerable pensioners, would they not face criminal charges for inciting a crime? Pembroke College is sadly far from alone. At Durham University, there is a drinking game called 'It's Only Rape If'.

An events company called the Varsity Leisure Group hosted students from Cardiff University and other local colleges at a fancy dress party. The theme? 'Pimps and Hoes'. 'CEOS and Hoes' is another popular party theme. At the University of Nottingham, there is a video on YouTube of young men singing:

These are the girls that I love best,

Many times I've sucked their breasts

Fuck her standing, fuck her lying,

If she had wings I'd fuck her flying

Now she's dead, but not forgotten,

Dig her up and fuck her rotten

This behaviour is not limited to the UK. At a Yale University fraternity, Delta Kappa Epsilon, in New Haven, Connecticut, members were captured on video chanting, 'No means yes! Yes means anal!' The frat house was suspended for five years but the damage was done. At St Mary's University in Canada, during 'Frosh Week' (their Freshers' Week), Frosh leaders were captured on video chanting, 'SMU boys like them young. Y is for your sister. O is for oh so tight. U is for underage. N is for no consent. G is for grab that ass.' Posters and T-shirts with 'I raped a woman last night and she cried' have been documented. You get the idea...

Now back to Freshers' Week where our kids will one day confront these offensive party themes and disrespectful slogans. We need to remind our teenagers that these first two weeks are meant to be an introduction to university life, clubs and to new friends, and warn them of the heavy drinking and safety concerns. We really feel strongly about empowering our young men and women to stand up against offensive behaviour. Obviously newcomers want to fit in to their new digs and social scene, but does this mean participating in activities they normally would not consider?

How many of our teens, pre-university, would attend a house party where the theme was, 'Pimps and Hoes' or 'Rappers and Slappers'? One daughter of a friend admitted with great embarrassment that when she and a girlfriend queued to get into a very 'hot' party, the doormen explained they had to 'flash their tits' in order to get in. They complied. Sexual harassment and laddish behaviour has become an accepted way of life at university. This attitude has incalculable long-term effects on how women view themselves in the broader context of their 'roles' in the world. Young women should not be accepting this behaviour or participating in events that are degrading to them. If they are taking off their clothes or performing lap dances to be accepted socially at an institution where they are supposed to be celebrated for their intellectual achievement, how will they view themselves in personal sexual relationships or in the work-force? And how does it shape the future husbands and fathers of our girls? And for those young men who enter the banking industry 'CEOs and Hoes' is not the right message, surely?

After speaking to sixth formers at a secondary school, a young woman asked us for advice on what to do about joining a popular dining society at her future uni. The problem was that the club called one event 'Slags'. Hmmm ... Well, it is pretty simple. We told her not to join. 'How prestigious can it be?' we asked. If you do not support these types of events then reason has it they are less likely to take place.

We have to consider, 'Does this behaviour encourage rape culture? Does it desensitise violence against women?' Gail Dines, author of *Pornland*, certainly believes the proliferation of hard-core pornography has an extremely negative influence on university students. The misogyny and objectification of young women as one-dimensional pieces of flesh do not help young men or young women develop healthy, intimate relation-ships with themselves or each other.

And yes, young men are also victims. There is a video on YouTube showing members of the University of Stirling hockey team loudly singing on public transportation. The lyrics are pretty disgusting, focusing on feeling up women, giving them their 'chunky' and worse. In the video, the drunken 'singers' are standing up and appear quite intimidating. Male and female passengers are visibly uncomfortable, some seen moving away from the louts and others audibly voicing their disgust. How could any young man stand up to this behaviour without fear of risking verbal or physical abuse? After we show our sixth form students this video, some of the guys laugh and the girls wince. But to be fair, many of the young men are pretty dis-gusted too. If our young people *are* shocked by this conduct, then where is it coming from? Perhaps it is a combination of social media, sexually explicit music videos and lyrics promot-ing violence against women, and the proliferation of hard-core pornography. How can we help our teenagers come to grips with this? By speaking to them and analysing specific instances of misogyny and homophobia.

Enter Dr Jackson Katz. Katz is one of the world's leading anti-sexist male activists, maker of the video 'Tough Guise: Violence, Media & the Crisis in Masculinity' and the Co-founder of Mentors in Violence Prevention. He has written many other books but what The RAP Project really loves about him is his 'bystander' message. According to Katz, the bystander is neither the victim nor the aggressor, but the person connected to the situation at hand. This could be the friends, teammates, schoolmates, teachers, etc. It asks how we, as a bystander, can speak up against sexual harassment and abuse. How can other men use this in particular to openly challenge this unacceptable behaviour? Katz shares this example. Imagine a group of guys at a poker table. Someone makes a derogatory or sexist comment. If the other players laugh, or say nothing at all, this can be taken as complicit to the sexism. If, however, someone takes the trouble to say they do not appreciate the comment and that the tasteless joke could be referring to his mother, sister or wife, their point may actually make an impact and inspire these people to think twice before making such derogatory comments.

The bystander approach is an attempt to empower people with the tools to interrupt this environment of complicity. Katz maintains that by speaking up, we are creating a climate where gender-based abuse is deemed unacceptable. It is morally wrong, and young men who behave this way will lose status and, hopefully, this behaviour will decrease as a result.

We go back now to the PPE's symposium on 'Tackling Rape, Sexual Assault and Harassment at Universities and Colleges'. Another of the speakers that made a positive impact was Dr Rachel Fenton, a Senior Lecturer of Law at the University of the West of England. She is also one of the leading developers of the 'Intervention Initiative', an online programme designed for university students and teachers aimed at decreasing incidents of rape, sexual assault and domestic abuse. The Intervention Initiative is a resource for universities and further education settings in England, developed in 2014 by the University of the West of England on receipt of a grant from Public Health England. It works by educating students to recognise and understand sexual and domestic violence and take active steps when they witness problematic behaviour. It takes a positive approach, encouraging all students to be active bystanders, standing up against any form of violence or abuse in their community. The eight-week online programme is designed to be delivered by experienced facilitators who help convey to students the necessary communication and leadership skills to intervene effectively and safely, and to change the social norm, making problematic violent behaviour socially unacceptable.

There are four stages to being a bystander in this approach:

- Notice an event taking place
- Interpret event as problematic
- Feel sense of responsibility for dealing with it
- Skills to act on the behaviour and assist victim

On the Intervention Initiative website, there is more information on how this programme works, including training and leadership advice, and the eight free sessions on skills, training, leadership, etc. Several UK universities are using this programme, including Bristol, the University of the West of England and SOAS, University of London.

We have spoken to freshers who have suggested that the victim of sexual harassment invite his or her harasser to the side, away from his or her group, and explain that this behaviour is not making you feel good and is very insulting. Most men, too, have said they prefer a one-to-one approach when ticking off a friend who is making an ass of himself.

We want to share with all parents the one thing we are absolutely sure about. We need to have this conversation at home, at the dinner table, in the car on the way to a match, with our sons and daughters, about Lad-itude. Let's ask them to define it, to explain where it might come from. Discuss with them how to identify it and what to do about it. Is it sports mentality, life on campus, popular mass culture or pornography? And let's share with them Katz's bystander approach. Let's not keep quiet but address the issue here and now.

We also believe men in power, professional athletes, politicians and celebrities have a unique opportunity to influence young people's attitudes and to be vocal about gender-based violence. Young men need role models, both on a personal level at home and on a larger social level. Think Ryan Gosling or Daniel Craig, as opposed to Dapper Laughs, the British comedian also known as Daniel O'Reilly, who promotes rape jokes. Katz believes our young men do not need 'sensitivity' training but 'leadership' training. Why not teach them at institutions of higher education, where our leaders and their policy are formed? Let's tackle these issues head-on, starting at home, promoting a mutual respect for young men and women.

UNIVERSITY

Understand the meaning of consent

Never open your front door to someone you do not know

Intervention Initiative: read about it

Vulnerable? Go easy. The first year can be tough

Enjoy yourself but don't overindulge

Report cases of sexual assault. Get help

Support your friends in times of need

Individuality: stay true to yourself

Try out different social clubs to get to know people

You need to practise safe sex. Really!

TOP TIPS

- Take some time to settle in. Relationships of all kinds will happen
- Get organised early on and stay focused
- Register with a local GP. Know the locations of campus police and medical facilities
- Only you and your housemates should have copies of the room key

Resources

Fenton, R, Mott, H and Rumney, P, 2015. A review of evidence for bystander intervention to prevent sexual and domestic violence in universities: Executive summary.

National Union of Students

www.nus.org.uk/en/campaigns/womens/

The Complete University Guide

www.thecompleteuniversityguide.co.uk/

The Intervention Initiative

http://www1.uwe.ac.uk/bl/research/interventioninitiative/support.aspx

theunipod

www.theunipod.com

Conclusion

The RAP Project began with questions. Do our children understand how complicated adolescence is when coupled with digital living online? Are they naïve? Do they realise posting suggestive pictures online or meeting someone they have met in a virtual world is illegal or possibly dangerous? These questions inspired more questions, and more and more young people appealed to us to address more and more issues they found challenging. We hope parents feel less uncomfortable asking some of the more awkward questions after reading this book. We are still asking them, and our teens, to continue to add more to the list.

Acknowledgements

We would like to share our heartfelt gratitude to the parents and teenagers who participated in our focus groups at the very beginning of our journey. To the teachers who first invited us in to speak to their students, who believed in us and continue to support our work, namely, Judith Prinsley, Peter Gittins, Sheena Moore, Anne Wakefield, James Harrison, Christiane Sitta and Ben de Jong.

Thank you to Daisy Goodwin who mentioned The RAP Project to her agent at Peters, Fraser & Dunlop. This in turn led to an introduction to our indomitable agent Nelle Andrew, who continued to guide us with her wisdom and experience. Without our editor at Penguin Random House, Morwenna Loughman, this book would not have been possible. Your brilliant, incisive and ever-positive disposition kept us going.

We would like to thank Becky Blaising, Tracey Marshall, Margot Simkin, Tom Rose, Julie Bentley, Dick Moore, Anthony Burton CBE, John Woolcombe and Martha Bolton.

Thank you to all of our interns who have worked very hard to enrich The RAP Project. Paolo and Talia, thank you. Your hard work proved invaluable with our work and our surveys. Our own teenagers' friends also provided invaluable information for this book, namely Kirsty, Andrew, Archie, Anya and Eliza.

Index

Appendix

FAQ

'My friend is posting revealing pictures of herself online and she won't stop. What can I do to help her stop? She is only 13.' *Please talk to an adult you trust who can help advise her on this. Remember it is against the law to post sexual images, texts or videos online under the age of 18.*

'A friend admitted he was the victim of a sexual assault. But he is too frightened to report it. I think he needs help as he is not himself'. *Encourage him to seek professional help from an organisation like Rape Crisis or Suvivors.Co.UK for example. The hope is that he or she will get enough support to report this crime.*

'I often hear people in the gym make rape jokes. My cousin was raped and when I hear these comments, I get upset.' *Rape jokes are unfortunately common. You may want to quietly tell the person making this 'joke' that rape is actually a violent crime which can emotionally damage a person for life, and your cousin certainly does not think it is funny.*

'If a girl is lying there drunk and mumbles 'yes', is that consent?' *If you are unsure as to whether someone wants to perform a sexual act with you, wait for them to show enthusiasm and give clear, verbal consent.*

'My child is getting bullied online and the posts are brutal. What can I do?' *Please take screenshots of the offensive posts and report them to your school's Head of Pastoral Care or to his or her Head of the school.*

The RAP Project Survey
3,000 Students aged 13–18 between 2015–2016

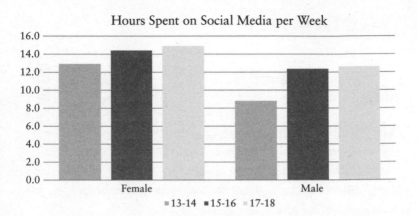

Hours Spent on Social Media per Week

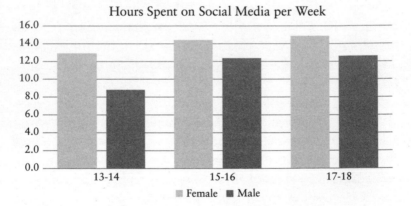

Hours Spent on Social Media per Week

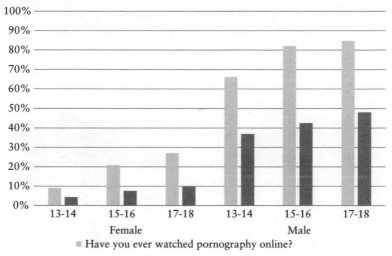

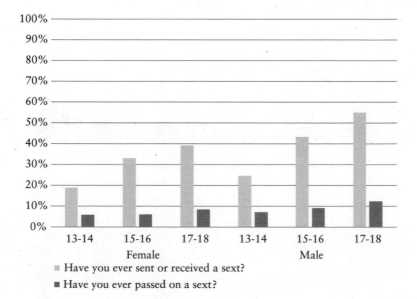

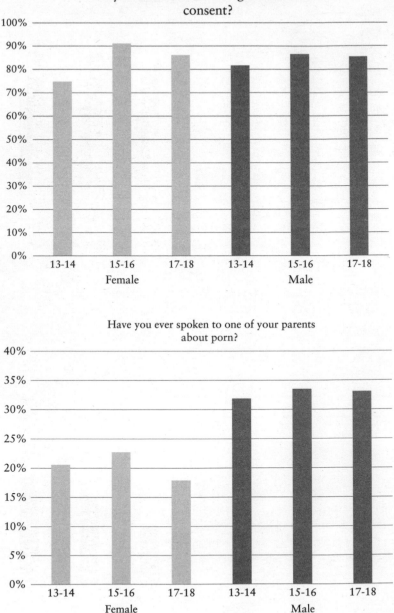

Have you experienced a clear example of sexism?

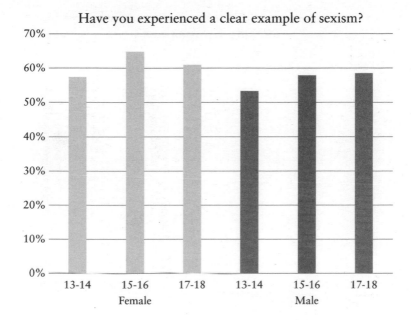

Have you ever used a dating app? i.e. Grindr or Tinder

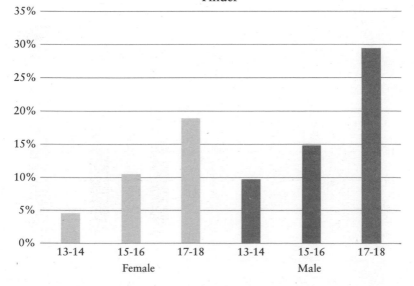

Have you ever done anything sexual while drinking that you regret?

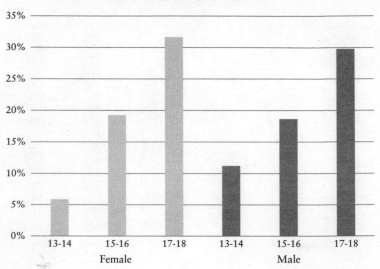